THE PAGAN EDEN:

ASSYRIAN ORIGINS

of the

KABBALISTIC TREE OF LIFE

The Assyrian Tree of Life

THE PAGAN EDEN:

ASSYRIAN ORIGINS

of the

KABBALISTIC TREE OF LIFE

The Assyrian Tree of Life

Ian Freer

AXIS MUNDI
BOOKS

Winchester, UK
Washington, USA

First published by Axis Mundi Books, 2013
Axis Mundi Books is an imprint of John Hunt Publishing Ltd., Laurel House, Station Approach,
Alresford, Hants, SO24 9JH, UK
office1@jhpbooks.net
www.johnhuntpublishing.com
www.axismundi-books.com

For distributor details and how to order please visit the 'Ordering' section on our website.

Text copyright: Ian Freer 2010

ISBN: 978 1 84694 504 5

A CIP catalogue record for this book is available from the British Library.

Design: Stuart Davies

Medical notice

This book is intended as an educational reference volume only and no part of it is intended as a medical manual. You must consult a qualified medical practitioner before taking or administering any substance mentioned in this book or mixing them with any current medication. If you suspect that you have a medical problem you should seek competent help. Advice from a qualified dietician or herbalist is recommended on matters relating to diet or herbs respectively.

Printed and bound by CPI Group (UK) Ltd, Croydon, CR0 4YY

We operate a distinctive and ethical publishing philosophy in all areas of our business, from our global network of authors to production and worldwide distribution.

CONTENTS

Acknowledgments

My wife Ramona has been devoted and supportive through thick and thin and her experienced editorial and literary advice, coming from an American perspective, has been invaluable; all remaining errors are mine. Some of the questions and answers raised in the book came from individuals who made comments or asked questions during my guided tours around the British Museum and my lectures on aspects of the subject. Suggestions from Ramona, Claire Wall, Mark Parry-Maddocks and Hanna Katz were gratefully received. I also wish to thank Rose Lopez for first bringing the Assyrian Tree theory to my attention by writing an article about it, Michael Baigent[4] and his sources for his vivid description of early Mesopotamian astrology in "From the Omens of Babylon" and numerous writers, researchers, teachers and practitioners in the areas under discussion, not least Professor Simo Parpola[5], without whom this book would be impossible and whose ingenuity, enormous learning, wisdom and technical expertise are a model for us all. Last, a sincere thank you to Rev. Maggy Whitehouse for suggesting my publisher and for the excellent work by all the team at my publisher.

Dedicated with love to Thomas and Sophie

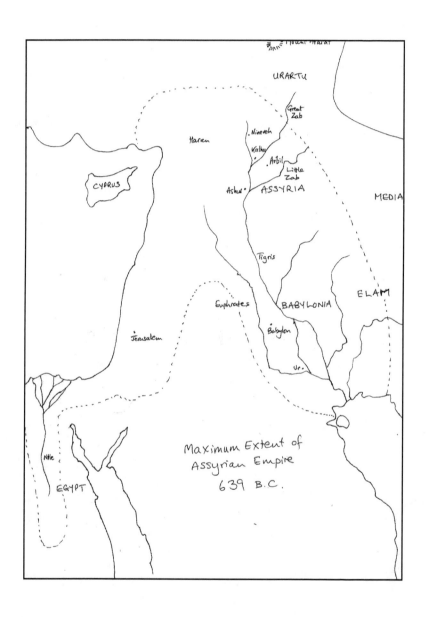

Introduction

This is an exploration in two main parts of how modern esoteric wisdom systems derive from ancient civilizations in and around the region that is now Iraq. The central theme is the connection between Heaven and Earth.

In the first part, the mystic Tree of Life, the central glyph of the Hebrew Kabbalah, turns out on investigation to **pre-date, perhaps by thousands of years, the origin of the Jewish people**, and in fact can be identified in the religious beliefs of another fascinating and much persecuted Semitic-speaking people, the Assyrians of Northern Iraq. The evidence for this astonishing deduction became public knowledge only at the end of the 20th century, after much study of the impressive palaces, fine artefacts, rediscovered language and fragmented legends of the Assyrians. The dating of the stylized tree with religious significance goes back to fourth-millennium Mesopotamia. This artistic Tree spread over the next two millennia to Egypt, Greece and the Indus Valley. The Tree of Life later appears in Christian, Jewish, Muslim and Buddhist art. In Kabbalah, this Tree is a kind of "map of God" and also of humanity; it has locations in it (called *sephiroth*), with detailed characteristics, such as colors and states of being, which can be explored by mystics to this day. The concept of the Sacred Tree of Life, occurring in various Holy Books, tends to unify or harmonize the world's main religions, just at a time in history when this is very desirable. (This is not my original theory but was first put forward in the Renaissance.)

Many authors claim that the written Kabbalah started in the Middle Ages (which is when the main text called the *Zohar* appeared) or possibly at around the time of Jesus (in reliance on older works like the *Hekhaloth* and *Merkavah* texts and *Sepher Yetzirah*); some writers note that Kabbalah means an *oral* tradition and that the Old Testament (the Jewish Bible) contains

Kabbalah and was written down some centuries earlier still. The new dating is very radical but it follows the earlier discovery of well-known similarities of some Mesopotamian Legends (e.g. the Flood) to certain stories in the Old Testament. I also discovered that the ancient Mesopotamians had an earlier version of the Garden of Eden story (called Inanna and the *Huluppu* Tree) featuring a goddess as the main character. There seems to be a deep connection between the Tree of Life in the Garden of Eden story and the mystic Tree of the Kabbalists.

Once I established a link between Heaven and Earth in the Tree symbol, I decided to look in the second part at what was in Heaven. The rationalistic science of astronomy, and its twin, the out of favour soul-science of astrology, also go back in clear, unbroken lineage to Mesopotamia but more specifically to the southern region, which was ruled first by the Sumerians and then by the Babylonians, before Western astrology spread around the world. (There may well be a separate root for Indian astrology and there certainly is for Chinese astrology.)

My investigations have revealed that both Astrology and Kabbalah are based on Number, which connects them in turn to the Greek philosopher Pythagoras. (In order to be absolutely clear, it was at around the time of Pythagoras that numbers started to become apparent in the surviving workings of Babylonian astrologers[1].) As Pythagoras was the main teacher in the earlier lineage of Socrates, Plato and Aristotle, it is arguable that the wider Near Eastern traditions have been the main source of all subsequent European philosophy and number-based sciences, such as arithmetic, geometry and the mapping of both time and space (cartography). Certainly the claims made for numerous scientific "firsts" in India would support the view that much of early European science came from the East.

Any references to astrology or astronomy in the ancient world actually mean the *same* subject, as they did not become separate in European thought until the Enlightenment. The 60 degree and

360 degree measurement system of hours or degrees, minutes and seconds, used today to measure both time and space, goes back to the counting system of Mesopotamia. This is encoded in the Kabbalistic Tree of Life, a statement that is proved later when we put Assyrian "deities" onto locations in the Sacred Tree. Furthermore, there is a case to be made for monotheism[2] in Assyria and Babylon, so there is no essential conflict at a deep level with the Jewish conception of the Tree as manifestations of the One True God. A different Hebrew name of God is given to each *sephirah* (the singular of *sephiroth* or location) on the Tree, thus adapting the Assyrian system to the Jewish.

(The argument for a monotheistic tendency in Babylonia is supported by a Spring Festival text of the High Priest chanting prayers to Marduk – the city god of Babylon - as the god who is immanent in all the planets, albeit under different names[3]. Also, a line in the Sumerian creation poem, the *Enuma Elish*, says, "Marduk, to Thee we have given kingship over the totality of the whole universe." Monotheistic tendencies are also discernible in Hindu scriptures and ancient Egyptian scriptures, although these traditions are often cited as examples of polytheistic traditions. The apparent dichotomy may be resolved if the unitary deity is seen as having different facets or dedicated conduits, hence, for example, the variety of "functional" saints within the Catholic Church tradition. This kind of approach could build a useful bridge between the two main traditions of Kabbalah.)

To the ancient peoples of Mesopotamia, leaders in world civilization in their heyday, Number had both a rational (quantitative) aspect and a mystical (qualitative) aspect. In modern Western science, the qualitative aspect has been hived off and labelled "numerology" or "sacred architecture" and so on; but in order to understand these people, we will need to bridge that gap and hold both aspects in play at the same time. Exercises in "mystical arithmetic" will be encountered as part of the reader's process of discovery. For example, the ancient Moon God had the

3

number 30, which can be subtracted from the number of another god to obtain a significant result. The value 30 is not arbitrary but probably relates to the days in the lunar month.

Obviously, the quantitative and qualitative values of Number suggest that different hemispheres of the brain are involved. By relating the two sides of the brain, we can help to harmonise its function and, I suggest, improve its efficiency.

My research also uncovered fascinating facts about the Kurds (who are descended from the ancient Hurrians, northern neighbours of the Assyrians) and how their traditional beliefs in Seven Angels have caused numerous "new" religious movements to arise in both the Near East and Europe; arguments for and against the existence of ancient telescopes; and many suggestive facts pointing to an ancient link between yoga and the other wisdom systems. By the end of this book you will also know that the concept of a Holy Trinity long pre-dates Christianity; and the Greek myths of the constellations actually go back originally to Sumer (or at least to somewhere on that same latitude).

Most surprising of all, I also found that there is a real "Tree of Life" in the natural world, long known by that title, a species whose leaves hold answers for many problems of contemporary medicine, including some thought to be otherwise virtually insoluble. Most of these medical discoveries, which are well documented by scientific papers, were made at the end of the 20th century. I thought this topic deserved an appendix on its own. So perhaps I found my Holy Grail while researching for this book. If so, I hope it will be equally life-enhancing to readers.

This is a specialist book. Readers who are new to the Kabbalah and/or Ancient Mesopotamia are advised to study introductory material first. Start with the Glossary of Terms, after which suggestions for further reading are included in the Bibliography and List of Websites, e.g. Halevi's *Kabbalah* and Hopking's *Practical Kabbalah Guidebook* . The Timeline sets out many of the major events in Mesopotamian and Kabbalistic history.

Nowadays, much useful reference material can be accessed online without charge (search under Kabbalah and Qabalah).

PART 1

NORTH:

THE ROOTS OF

THE TREE OF LIFE

Chapter One

Two Systems and Two Rivers

What is the connection between the unspecified Tree of Life in the Bible story of the Garden of Eden and the schematic Tree of Life in Qabalah? What were they? Where might they come from in history? How do they link Heaven and Earth? These are the central questions I set out to answer in this book.

I have been studying astrology and Qabalah under various teachers for some thirty years now. I should start by defining these terms. These are symbolic systems of wisdom. Some readers may be under the misapprehension, from newspaper astrology, that astrology is simply a forecasting system of dubious validity. In fact it is a subtle and complex technical method for analysing trends in human nature and behaviour, based mainly on numerical relationships between planetary positions, which we might call Pythagorean. You can throw out zodiac signs and houses, as some astrologers do, but the core is there in the aspects (angles of significant degrees apart) and configurations between planets. It is a form of planetary numerology.

Similarly, in Qabalah, (the Western or Christian term for studies based on Jewish Kabbalah) we have a focus on planets and number in relationship. The modern Golden Dawn or Hermetic style of Qabalah (a phenomenon of the Gentile world), using the Tarot on the paths of the Tree of Life diagram, attributes *sephiroth* (the various locations on the Tree) to planets and other correspondences. Paths connect the *sephiroth*. Both paths and *sephiroth* have numerical values. The Tree shows that the divine nature is both a unity and many-faceted. As the Kabbalah is a system of theosophy (god-wisdom), the *sephiroth* are various archetypes or principles of the divine Godhead and the Tree diagram is simply a set of *sephiroth* arranged geometrically in three columns with straight connecting paths between them. The central *sephirah* of Tifereth or Beauty is particularly important and expresses the divine principle of Love, central to so many spiritual paths. Why that should be so, in historical terms, is demonstrated in this book.

Secret texts from ancient Babylon detail the mystic numbers associated with each god, the plants, the metals, the precious and semi-precious stones, in other words a variety of correspondences. The texts always end: "A secret of the great gods. May the initiate instruct the initiate. Let the uninitiated not see."[6] This tradition has continued directly into the modern world. Everyone who knows their zodiac sign will have seen gift shop items which state which stone is linked to that sign. You can buy books of "correspondence lists". Some relate to the Kabbalistic Tree of Life. Others relate to astrology. I have even seen books on the yoga chakras pursuing this theme.

The concept is the same. All of the universe resonates or vibrates. The frequencies connect everything on the same level of correspondence and frequency is a manifestation of number. This Law of Resonance is a basic law of Tantric Yoga and Qabalah (I have heard the latter described as "Jewish Tantra"). One consequence of this law is that whatever you focus your intention upon will tend to be drawn into your life[7]. You must pay careful watch not only to your words but even to your thoughts, which precede them. Intention is the key because thought determines action, at least to the extent that we have free will. This is a key practical benefit of studying such systems.

Even the most rational and skeptical reader would probably agree that thought or intention largely determines action. This is, for example, a basic truism of every legal system, so obvious that it does not need to be stated. Scientists will also agree that resonance or vibration is a characteristic of matter, since the advent of wave theory from quantum mechanics. My statements are extrapolations of commonly held intellectual assumptions that are, not coincidentally, also found in ancient wisdom traditions. I have lost count of the number of writers who state "my tradition has always held such-and-such to be the case and now modern science agrees at last." It certainly underlines the truth that our ancestors were just as intelligent as we are.

You don't have to believe in any mystical system to see that Number is the basis of everything. Scientists say that all the known elements can be arranged in a periodic table based on number. They also say that the planetary orbits in the solar system are arranged in ever-increasing distances based on Number, so that unknown planets have actually been discovered by looking in the expected area. This principle is called Bode's Law and has been current science for centuries. There is one planet, Neptune, which seems to break the sequence, but otherwise it holds up fairly well and, given the massive size of the bodies involved, it is hard to ascribe to mere random coincidence. If you wish to explore this avenue more deeply, I recommend to you the works of astrologer-mathematician Robin Heath, a man who knows how many significant numbers are found both in the megaliths and in the cosmos to which their builders aligned them.

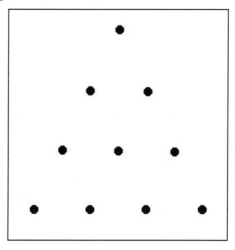

I mentioned earlier the word *Pythagorean*. Pythagoras was a Greek philosopher and mathematician who studied in the ancient Near East. He was a vegetarian, reincarnationist and leader of a mystic community, who probably looked and taught much like one of the yogis of India. He is best remembered for popularizing the Music of the Spheres, the supposed celestial harmony of the planets (in other words, manifestations of Number in the cosmos). He also left us a diagram called the Tetractys, which shows the relationship between the numbers four and ten. A series of ten points are arranged in a pyramid of base 4, next level 3, next level 2 and final level 1.

Qabalists who see that diagram will immediately think of the Tree of Life diagram. Why? The Tree of Life consists of a series of 10 *sephiroth* or divine emanations from the Godhead, Ain Soph, through the Four Worlds of Emanation, Creation, Formation and Action. This is a more detailed model of what I stated earlier about intention preceding action. Some Tree of Life diagrams show 40 sephiroth, the 10 sephiroth in 4 worlds. This is known as the Extended Tree. All based on that tetractys of Pythagoras, one might reasonably assume.

This topic is discussed at some length by the American academic, John Opsopaus, in his companion book to the Pythagorean Tarot. His Pythagorean Tarot deck is written in Greek. It strips out medieval Christian thought from the Tarot and goes further back to the Classical numerology of pagan Greek philosophy. He sets out various interesting connections between the thinkers of Ancient Greece and their precursors in the Near East. There is cogent evidence from ancient writers (themselves from the Near East) that Pythagoras did indeed study there.

I am not certain that Pythagoras can properly be described as a Kabbalist or a Yogi but he had many common interests with them. He was certainly a mystic who studied sacred number and believed in karma and reincarnation. His teaching organisation was similar to the schools of Master Kabbalists and of Hindu Yogis or Gurus.

There is some backwards influence which needs to be taken into account; the important early Kabbalistic book, the Sepher Yetzirah or Book of Formation, is clearly influenced by Pythagoras and not the other way round. (This is discussed by Opsopaus[8] and also by Kaplan in his introduction to the *"Sefer Yetzirah"*).[9] The other interesting point I would make about the antecedents of Pythagoras is that he possibly met with a Druid called Abaris although there is no classical reference for this belief[10]; and the Druids were known as skilled astronomers and reincarnationists (I know of numerous classical sources for this description).

Returning to the Tetractys: the numbers 4 and 10 are also fundamental to the Tarot. There are 4 suits and 10 numbers in each suit, just as in an ordinary deck of playing cards. There are 22 Trumps, just as there are 22 letters in the Hebrew alphabet. There is no reason to believe that it was designed with the Kabbalah in mind, despite many intriguing similarities, and that line of enquiry must be speculative. In fact an entirely different explanation of the Tarot's origins is given by Opsopaus, namely a derivation from the ancient game of knucklebones (dice)[11].

Please bear in mind that in traditional Jewish Kabbalah there were many ways of drawing the Tree of Life diagram, sometimes inverted from the usual, so that the paths vary in number and location, thus tending to undermine the "ancient Kabbalah" theory of the origin of Tarot.

The fields of study pursued among Kabbalists have included reincarnation, eternal life, the path of the lightning flash, guardian angels, numerology, amulets, gods and demons, meditation, prayer, incense, ritual, symbols, codes, and much more. It is very significant for the argument of this book that all those matters were known in ancient Assyria. Just note for now that some of them are outside the scope of Orthodox Jewish religious belief; but there was no such thing in existence when they first came together, because that period pre-dated the origin of the Jewish identity. Many readers may assume that the Jewish tradition originates only in Israel (because there is so much emphasis on that land from the time of Moses onwards) and possibly Egypt (because of the famous Exodus story). However, the world of Mesopotamia was equally important to the Jews at the time the Old Testament was written down and afterwards, because many Jews had been taken into captivity and some of their descendants remained there in large numbers even after they were permitted to return to Israel. It is probably true to say that, in the early centuries of the Common Era, Mesopotamia was the world center of Jewry. This is arguably why, for example, Mesopotamian style astrology (and the Aramaic rather than Hebrew script) features in a number of books of the famous Dead Sea Scrolls, written down by religious Jews (not by Christians) a little over 2,000 years ago.

How far back does all this really go? The kind of astrology, with signs and houses, which we use today, coalesced little more than 2,000 years ago but it came from much earlier Babylonian astronomy and omen techniques. It has roots at the beginning of urban civilisation in Mesopotamia. The very first culture there is called Sumerian but more properly we should speak of the land of Shumer (the Biblical land of Shinar). This was the first urban civilization to appear in what is now Iraq and it was based in the south-east of that country, around the lower reaches of the two rivers Tigris and Euphrates, facing the coast.

The best known Sumerian today, judging from the remains found in museums, is a nobleman called Gudea, who lived more than 4,000 years ago. You can see images of him in the British Museum and in the Louvre. He ruled a Sumerian city called Lagash. He had an astrological dream. The gods appeared to him and told him where to build a certain temple, in a position based on the placement of the planets. We know that the Sumerians worshipped many gods, some of whom were astral, that is to say linked to - but not the same as - heavenly bodies. These were celestial correspondences.

Where did the Sumerians come from? They may have always been where we found them but Samuel Noah Kramer wrote in 1983[12] that the Sumerians did not arrive in the land, which was already occupied by a people described as the Ubaidians, until the second half of the fourth millennium BC, and he suggested that, as their language was an agglutinative tongue, like that of the Turkic peoples, they may have come from south-central Asia. I have checked and found that there are many other agglutinative languages recorded, probably coincidentally, so this is not a strong hypothesis. Their legends refer to a land of origin called *Dilmun*, which is now believed by some to be centered on the Gulf state of Bahrein, due to excavations carried out there in the 1950s by the Danish archaeologist, Geoffroy Bibby (according to Michael Baigent[13], although Kramer has described Dilmun as unidentified[14]).

The Sumerians had colonies around the Gulf (e.g. at Oman, Kuwait, Qatar, Abu Dhabi and another site some 200 miles inside Saudi Arabia) and traded with the early Indian civilization in the Indus Valley, which had a different written language. The Indus Valley (close by the area of the lost river Saraswati, also found in modern Pakistan) is the first great river valley to the east, because mountains lie in between. (The accepted academic view is that the proto-Sanskrit of the Indus valley was influenced by the script of Sumer, which makes me wonder what other areas of influence we can determine. Interestingly, the script of the Indus Valley appears to correlate with the script of Easter Island in the Pacific Ocean[15].) All of these civilisations stored water in large quantities, sometimes underground, sometimes overground. Mesopotamia, for example, was riddled with canals in addition to its two mighty rivers which were used like motorways.

Unlike the Sumerians, it is widely held that the first urban people in the Indus Valley were more Tantric than Vedic in emphasis (although the distinction is not easy to make and is artificial according to White[16]). This meant that they had no centralized kings or chief priests and therefore no great palaces or temples (or at least none discovered so far). They allegedly worshipped privately their version of Shiva and Shakti, the male and female principles of consciousness and energy, as honored and invoked for "kundalini" energy work in Tantric Yoga. Lord Shiva at that time was a moon deity, which is why he is always shown in contemporary religious art as pale coloured and linked with the crescent moon and a horned beast. (See appendix 1 for a fuller account of Shiva, yoga and the fascinating link with the Gundestrup Cauldron, often hailed as a masterpiece of Celtic art[17].)

I mention these Indian concepts because they are better understood than Sumerian beliefs and show us a wider pattern. At this early phase of urban development, humanity was linking religion in part to bodies in the heavens. The great goddess of the Sumerians, Inanna[18], was linked to Venus as was her later successor Ishtar of Babylon. In other words, these people had a partly *astral religion*.

The Sumerian pantheon starts with elder gods, which we might call gods of the four elements, but the subsequent generations related to the moon, Sun and planets. They believed in a sky god An, an earth goddess Ki (later Ninhursag), the air god Enlil and the water god Enki (Ea). An and Ki are the primordial pair and can be compared with the concepts of Yang and Yin respectively in Taoism (there is even some similarity in the words themselves). Enlil is the offspring of these two and Enki (Ea) is sometimes called the son of An. In the next generation, the Moon God, Nanna, fathers both the Sun god, Utu, and the goddess of the planet Venus, Inanna.

Ea or Enki is a particularly hard figure to grasp unless we have a Kabbalistic context. In Kabbalah he relates to the sephirah

of Wisdom (Chokmah), which lies directly above an abyss occupied by Da'ath (Knowledge), which means esoterically that you cannot attain Wisdom without first attaining Knowledge (which implies teaching, a guide offering a bridge over the abyss).

Ea was sometimes called the antelope of the *Abzu* (freshwater abyss) which might explain the famous goat-fish representations of Ea, now linked to the astrological sign of Capricorn. This mixed-up creature, ascribed in legend to a time of chaos, shows esoterically that he is master of two elements, almost a Freudian map of the visible conscious and hidden unconscious elements of the mind. One of the god's other symbols was a "curved stick" (so-called) terminating in a ram's head. This is a very obscure symbol and cannot be astrological since there was no ram in the original Mesopotamian zodiac (the constellation we know as Aries was instead known as The Hireling). There is however a striking connection here with Hindu Lord Shiva:

(1) The River Ganges flows from Shiva's hair, just as fresh water, sometimes containing fishes, flows from Ea.
(2) Shiva or Cernunnos on the Gundestrup Cauldron lifts a ram-headed snake.
(3) Both are represented as seated gods.
(4) Both are associated with wisdom.

(5)   Ea uses incantations and Shiva uses mantras.

(6)   Ea's city of Eridu was closest of all Sumerian cities to the Persian Gulf and therefore to the Indus Valley.

I am certain that the concept of the abyss in Kabbalah comes directly from the Sumerian concept of the subterranean freshwater abyss or *Abzu*. According to the Babylonian account of Creation, *Enuma Elish*, the only creatures in existence at the beginning of the world were Tiamat, the female sea, and Apsu (i.e. *Abzu*), the male fresh waters. They produced offspring by mingling their waters together, which produced the younger gods. Apsu plotted to kill them all (echoed in later Greek myth) but this led to the killing of Apsu by Ea and of Tiamat by Marduk. Professor Simo Parpola of Helsinki University has demonstrated that the Kabbalistic Tree of Life is a family tree of the gods, from an Assyrian perspective, which is his specialist subject, but here we have an exciting indication that it may go back as far as the Sumerians (See also in chapter 3 the Sumerian story of Inanna and the *Huluppu*-tree).

The Sumerians had a legendary wise man called Adapa[19]. As a sage or *apkallu* of Eridu, the earliest city in Sumer, he had wisdom and position granted by the god Ea (as we have seen, the god of fresh water[20] or *abzu* and also associated with magic and the arts and skills of civilisation). Having "broken the wings of the south wind", Adapa was summoned for punishment by the supreme god, Anu. Ea had told Adapa that he would be offered the bread and water of death. Meanwhile the two gatekeepers of heaven had interceded with Anu, who had a change of heart. Anu instead offered the sage the bread and water of eternal life (the proto-Christian symbolism here is extraordinary). Of course, Adapa refused, thus losing the chance of immortality. The Sumerians had a keen sense of irony.

At the end of his days, Adapa ascended into heaven and became angelic. Adapa is a likely model for the long-lived concept of "guardian angels" that first appear in our culture holding buckets and standing by the Tree of Life in Assyrian art. This proves that there is nothing at all "New Age" about such a concept – it is very ancient. Adapa is the precursor of a figure important to Kabbalists, the patriarch Enoch, who is supposed to have been taken up to heaven and gradually lost his human characteristics and became the angel Metatron, who, according to Kabbalistic tradition, stands before the throne of the Almighty (as the Greek root of his name would suggest). The reference here is to the Merkabah Book of Enoch, also known as 3 Enoch or Sefer Hekhalot. There is a whole fascinating tradition of lost ancient scientific knowledge around Enoch, which has been explored and published by Christopher Knight and Robert Lomas under the title *"Uriel's Machine"*. The Machine was an astronomical measuring device and its story overlaps with mine in a number of places.

The Sumerians spoke and wrote in a language that has no known relatives (as the various agglutinative languages found in the Basques and Chechens, for example, appear to be unrelated to each other, according to linguists). This makes them very mysterious and intriguing. One of their words we all know: Eden was their name for the fertile plains that lay between the Tigris and the Euphrates. (In fact Assyria was the most fertile region of the two because it did not need all the great canals and irrigation channels that were constructed further south. The drawback to that was that invaders came along rather frequently.) The Sumerians had a status like the Romans had in the Middle Ages, seen as a great force in the past which had left a legacy used by other people.

This river system in Mesopotamia was their equivalent of a motorway network. If you extend the area westwards to Israel and Egypt, you have a region often described as "the fertile crescent". In the period we are considering, it was much more fertile than it is now. The desert has encroached since then and other regions have prospered instead. The loss of local kings to oversee maintenance and the over-use of irrigation channels in ancient Iraq led to the water table becoming so saline that eventually the cities had to be abandoned. New cities later on, such as Baghdad, led a resurgence that continued through the Middle Ages but the old cities became dusty mounds or "tells" within the last 2,000 years.

The Sumerians were ultimately supplanted by a very prolonged and slow immigration of Semites from the Arabian Peninsula. These Semites introduced a new language called Akkadian, otherwise known as Eastern Semitic. It is in the same family as Arabic, Hebrew and Aramaic (the latter was the language of Syrian tribes people, naturally spoken by Jesus as it was from the first millennium BC the main regional language of the Fertile Crescent, prior to the Muslim introduction of Arabic). Akkadian was split into two dialects, Babylonian in the south and Assyrian in the north. The dialects were close enough that if you spoke one you could follow the other. The language is called Akkadian by scholars, after King Sargon of Agade, who was an early Semitic conqueror. The Babylonians were the predominant civilization in the 2nd millennium BC. For a few centuries early in the 1st millennium BC the Assyrians ruled the Fertile Crescent, followed by a brief neo-Babylonian Empire which was in turn toppled permanently by the Persians.

The Semitic family of languages is a very interesting one. The Arabian peninsula has produced wave after wave of new populations who spoke new forms of the Semitic languages, named after the Biblical character Shem. Although we often use the term anti-Semitism to mean prejudice against Jews alone, there are plenty of other nations who speak Semitic languages and it has been proven that, for example, the Israelis and Palestinians have the same DNA. In the modern world, Arabic is the most widely used Semitic language, and this trend is certain to increase.

At the time of Jesus, the Islamic religion did not yet exist, and the great movement of peoples which spread it around much of the world had not yet started and so Arabic was confined to Arabia. Instead, the common tongue then was a Semitic language with its own alphabet, which came from the Bedouin Aramaeans of Syria, called Aramaic. Jesus would have spoken Aramaic, Greek and perhaps also Latin. Aramaic is very similar to Akkadian but started to replace it during the 1st millennium BC. The main reason for this was the expansion of the Assyrian and Babylonian Empires, whose success drew in neighbouring peoples. Furthermore, they were quite capable of relocating entire groups of people within their Empire, just as Stalin did later in Soviet Russia.

The Aramaic alphabet replaced the old cuneiform writing in time, which must have been a great help as it was much simpler. Cuneiform died out slowly and was still being read by Ptolemy (2nd century AD). The cuneiform scripts required hundreds or even thousands of wedge patterns to be memorised, a deterrent to all but a few. This would have kept the literacy rate very low, even without the challenging problem of having to translate earlier texts from the unrelated language of the Sumerians.

The introduction of a short alphabet was definitely helpful to all the peoples who adopted it. The Semitic-speaking Phoenicians (a great trading nation on the coast of modern Lebanon and Syria, who founded the Carthaginian Empire) were probably the first to do so, quickly followed by such nations as the Greeks and the Hebrews. The Greeks and Hebrews adopted an alphabet *before* they gave numerical values to the letters (the dating is given by Opsopaus for those who are interested). It was however only a matter of time before convenience led to the use of letters as numbers, e.g. Alpha for 1, Beta for 2 and so on. This is the origin of what we call the "Greek Kabbalah" with its parallel application in Hebrew; it simply means using words of equal numerical value to discover real or imaginary hidden meanings.

This was the first attempt at "deep language" as an intellectual endeavour.

Incidentally, one of the curiosities of Kabbalah is the assertion in the *Zohar* that the alphabet was created first of all creation – clearly this cannot be literally true but it may convey the concept that the truths or energies embodied by the letters (in their mystical aspect) were divine and therefore created at a very early stage indeed. This is how I, at any rate, have tried to make sense of the belief. The *Zohar* was written down long after Pythagoras and his lineal follower Plato lived, so it is tempting to see the influence of Plato's theory of *Forms* or *Archetypes*, made popular in the modern world by C.G.Jung. If we look upon the Kabbalistic letters as expressions of "archetypal" energy, then it begins to make much more sense.

Professor Simo Parpola of the University of Helsinki has been publishing on Assyriology for over three decades at the time of writing. He originated the theory of the Assyrian Qabalistic Tree of Life, first given in a lecture and then published in an extensive survey published in the *Journal of Near Eastern Studies*, Volume 52(2), 1993, at pp.161-298. Some brief information from this article was also published in John Opsopaus' book on the Pythagorean Tarot. The chief connection between the two writings is the mystical study of number, which I turn to next.

Key points

- Kabbalah originated in Assyria, thousands of years before the modern era and before the Jewish identity.
- Astrology was the same subject as astronomy and the unbroken lineage is traceable back to Sumer.
- There is some sort of link between "sacred number", Pythagoras and these Near East traditions; but it is complex due to international travel.
- The Tarot card deck was invented in the Middle Ages; it

does not derive from Kabbalah but may well be influenced somehow by Pythagoras.

- Pythagoras propounded an arithmetical diagram called the Tetractys which looks Kabbalistic.
- The Sumerian sage Adapa is the precursor of the Hebrew sage Enoch also known as the Angel Metatron.
- The Semitic family of languages produced a written alphabet which only later had numerical values attached (in the case of Hebrew) with a parallel development in Greek.

Chapter 2

It's All Done By Numbers

Opsopaus discusses how, in the Greek Qabalah, the name of a god like Apollo had a numerical equivalent (alpha = one, etc.) so that temples to the gods used measurements that corresponded to the value of that godname[21]. He says this practice originated in Assyria. Its technical name is *Isopsephia* which equates to *gematria*/geometry (literally: *earth measuring*).

Parpola devotes space to the numerical values of the Assyrian godnames and the epithets of the gods. From this he derived a scheme which allows him to place them on the three pillars of the Tree of Life. Not surprisingly, at this very earliest stage it does not have the same correlations to planetary gods that we have now. Thus the Moon God Sin is placed by Parpola at Binah, not Yesod, and Venus/Ishtar is at Tiphereth, not Netzach.

The sephirothic meanings are in any case not the same as those of the planets attributed by many modern Qabalists. If you are used to a different scheme of correspondences, I ask that you put this on one side, just for now, as the reason for the difference will become apparent later. (I could give a very detailed list of epithets which justify these correspondences but I do not want to overwhelm the reader with detail in this introductory level book.)

In Hebrew the meaning of *sephirah* is "counting"[22] or "number," but not, as some have suggested, sphere or sapphire or pomegranate, and certainly not planet. (When you look at corresponding planets you add a whole new layer of correspondences, and we aren't in that period yet.) This "counting" of the sephiroth may have been quite literally done on the fingers.

This was, for example, how the Druids used their Ogham language (a tally system written in base 5) according to the

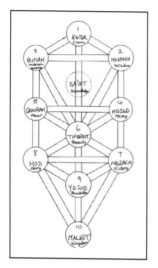

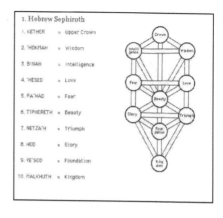

1. Hebrew Sephiroth

1. KETHER	=	Upper Crown
2. 'HOKMAH	=	Wisdom
3. BINAH	=	Intelligence
4. 'HESED	=	Love
5. PA'HAD	=	Fear
6. TIPHERETH	=	Beauty
7. NETZA'H	=	Triumph
8. HOD	=	Glory
9. YE'SOD	=	Foundation
10. MALKHUTH	=	Kingdom

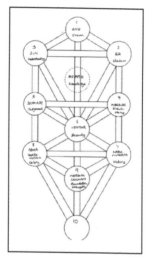

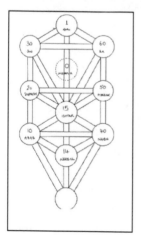

medieval Irish text[23], the *Book of Ballymote*. It is a striking parallel that the Druids themselves had an oral tradition, for the ban on writing was widely observed. Sources say that they wrote in Greek when they had to do so. Ellis laments the destruction of Druidical books in Ireland by zealot Christian missionaries.[24]

This was in marked contrast to the Christian monks who had a sacred book, the Bible, and devoted their lives to writing it out again and again. The Christian influence on former Druid cultures meant that the writing ban was eventually lifted, so that from the early Christian period we have monumental inscriptions on marker stones, in Ireland and Wales particularly. These are in the Goidelic language of Ireland, using Ogham script on the corners of the stones. (The concept of marker stones is perhaps more familiar from the Babylonian *kudurru* or boundary stones, as seen on display in the British Museum and elsewhere.) As the Druidic roots of Celtic Christianity withered over time, so the use of Ogham declined, aided by deliberate destruction.

From the process of attributing gods to sephiroth, Professor Parpola derives a meaning to the designation of positive and negative pillars. See the series rising by 10 working up the left or negative pillar and then continuing up the right or positive pillar. If you subtract any left-hand sephirah from the right-hand sephirah at that level, the result is always 30. The total value of the middle pillar by addition is also 30.

The practice of writing divine names with numbers emerged under the Middle Assyrian Empire and represents a genuinely Assyrian innovation. This was in the early 13th century BC and thus coincides with the abstract Late Assyrian Tree. I appreciate the fact that the Moon God's number is 30 which is a rounded up lunar month in days. The supreme god's number is 1, as you would expect.

The total number of the individual sephiroth is 240. Remember that figure. Now find the total for the middle pillar (30) and each pair of opposites by subtracting the left number from the right number. This gives 4 x 30 = 120. Add that 120 to the 240 (which I asked you to remember). The total is 360, the number of days in an Assyrian year and the circumference of the universe expressed in degrees. Remember that Mesopotamians loved numbers based on 60 and 360.

Professor Parpola sees the Tree as a symbol of the Assyrian King himself. The familiar Kabbalistic "Microcosmic Man" shown with the Tree of Life superimposed on his standing body was none other than Ashurbanipal or one of his lineage! The bearded Assyrian King is, I suggest, an archetypal image for patriarchal deity in this region and this would help to explain why later Qabalistic writers found mystical value in such odd exercises as counting the hairs in the divine beard – see, for example, S.L.MacGregor Mathers's translations of portions of the Zohar, titled "The Kabbalah Unveiled".[25]

The first sephirah is called Kether the Crown, which implies kingship. The final or tenth sephirah is called Malkuth, the Kingdom, which also fits this interpretation, and it is often shown as four differently colored sections, which again connects 4 to 10. This is however a fundamental relationship in the human psyche. Look at your fingers. You have 10 digits but only 4 fingers on each hand and you have 4 limbs. It would be hard for Pythagoras not to have noticed that.

Qabalists have claimed that above Kether lies a mysterious source of the divine emanations, called Ain Soph Aur or limitless light. By a Qabalistic technique of wordplay called Notarikon, in which each letter of a word stands for a whole word, Parpola derives Ain Soph Aur from the letters of Ashur, the state god of Assyria. This would fit with his scheme because Ashur is the only major god NOT tied to any sephirah.

Ashur was both the capital city and state god[26]. Assyria is simply our form of this word and it survives in the name of the modern state of Syria[27] (which was once the western region of Greater Assyria). Ashur was usually shown as a winged disc in

Assyrian art. Sometimes streamers of lightning emanate downwards. So if Ashur is at the top of the Tree diagram, no wonder we have the path of the Lightning Flash below.

Professor Parpola has argued that just as later Kabbalists paid attention to the esoteric meanings of the divine name YHWH, so the Assyrians must have had a great esoteric tradition concerning Ashur/Assur. They did so in relation to other deities so their supreme deity, *a fortiori*, would have received similar study. He lists five principal spellings of Ashur's name and interprets them as follows:

The One
The Only One
Mystery
The Perfect One
God is One
The Only God
The Hidden God
A Single Flash
The First Flash
Flashing Water
Flowing Waters
Totality of Heaven
Totality of Gods
Universal God
God is Many

The Ain Soph Aur of the Kabbalists is shown in three distinct phases:

Ain – Nothingness
Ain Soph – Limitlessness
Ain Soph Aur – Limitless Light

After these phases, the sephiroth emanate from Kether to Malkuth (perhaps derived from An and Ki respectively) in a sequence known as the Lightning Flash. All of these concepts find resonance in the names of Ashur/Assur.

Alan Millard, Rankin Professor of Hebrew and Ancient Semitic Languages at the University of Liverpool, has described how, in the world of Mesopotamia, oral compositions used similarities of sound in various ways for effect and to aid memorization[28]. Writing simply expanded these possibilities. Mesopotamian scribes wrote riddles and developed devices like acrostics, so that taking the first sign of each line of a text produced a sentence, even giving an author's name. This technique will be very familiar to Kabbalists. Some words and divine names, as we have seen, had numerical values. Alphabetic acrostics occur in several *Psalms*, e.g. 37 and 119 and the *Book of Lamentations*. The prophecy of *Jeremiah 25;26* includes a code whereby Babylon (bbl) becomes Sheshach (ssk) on the system A=Z, B=Y etc. which readers of *The Da Vinci Code* may recognise as the *Atbash Cipher* which is a genuine Hebrew cryptography technique or substitution cipher. (The use of mystical numbers continued into the New Testament, e.g. in *Revelation* where 7 and 666 both have esoteric significance.)

At an early stage in the evolution of the Tree diagram in Assyrian art, it developed a triadic structure. It did this first in Assyria. The abstract and harmonious triadic structure is a hallmark of the subsequent Qabalistic Tree of Life. It is not surprising that triads developed because the Mesopotamian religion had a holy trinity consisting (if I may paraphrase with the more familiar Christian terms) of the moon as God the Father, the Sun as God the Son and Venus as the Holy Spirit. These were major deities among some 3,000 deities, mostly not of an astral nature at all.

Many people have asked me, why was the moon the ruler of the triad? I have two answers: the first, an aesthetic point, is that the Mesopotamians, like the Canaanites, had a partly astral religion, tied up to an extent with the stars and the seasons and calendar, so the brightest body in the night sky would be seen as ruler; the second, a scientific one, is that the moon was used as a measure of the calendar, and was much more useful for this purpose than any other body.

A related question is: why is Venus in the triad at all? She is the only true planet included. The mythological answer to why Venus is in the triad is that it is a family tree of gods, for the moon is parent to both Sun and Venus. The astronomical answer would be that she is the brightest of all the planets because her orbit comes closest to that of the earth. She has a dual nature as evening star or morning star and sometimes disappears for months on end. The adjective "inconstant" as applied to the moon might be applied to Venus with far greater accuracy. The moon is so very constant that she is the basis of much early astronomy and an essential part of calendar calculation. The puzzle of calculating where Venus would be next was very important to early astronomers, as we shall see later on.

The triad pattern is also used in the Tantric tradition. If we set up a spiritual goal, for example, the attainment of bliss, it is in practice impossible to proceed without considering also the obstacles to bliss. These obstacles set up a polarity before us. It is a horizontal polarity. The solution given in the Tantric tradition (by oral teachings) is to transcend vertically above this duality and find a resolution at the next level. There is something on the next level which will bring them together and end the apparent conflict. This type of approach is also used by Western Qabalists when they work through triads on the Tree of Life. Modern philosophers have used a similar triadic technique of thesis, antithesis and synthesis.

The Tree is also a *Family Tree* because the lineage flows downwards on the side pillars. For example, Sin is the father of both Shamash and Ishtar, placed immediately below him. The full sequence supplied by Professor Parpola in his seminal article is:

1. An/Anu, father of Ea
2. Ea, brother of Enlil
3. Nanna/Sin, son of Enlil
4. Marduk (son of Ea) or Enlil
5. Shamash, son of Sin
6. Ishtar, daughter of Sin
7. Nabu (son of Marduk) or Ninurta (son of Enlil)
8. Adad was either son of Enlil (early) or An/Anu (later)
9. Nergal (brother of Ninurta)

Even though Adad does not obviously fit below Shamash in order of descent, they are nevertheless all related and all in chronological order in this scheme. It is also interesting that the final three gods, Ninurta, Adad and Nergal, had some unattractive aspects which would be appeased rather than adored, culminating in entry to the underworld itself, ruled by Nergal. He was often addressed in prayers and hymns intended to avert the associated dangers. Nergal was seen as a fallen sky god who visited the underworld as a punishment and stayed with Ereshkigal thereafter. As he is also a god of light, it is tempting to compare him with the later concept of the angel Lucifer.

The sequence of gods in the creation myth can be translated into numbers in the same way. It appears to be a code. In the text *Enuma Elish*, Anu is born and then creates Ea which is called "his likeness". Professor Parpola suggests that this is a reference to the fact that the mystic numbers of these two gods, 1 and 60, were written with the same sign. The sequence of creation was that nothingness was replaced by oppositions and the infinite universe (Ansar = Assur) with its negative counterpart (Kisar = limited physical space). Assur emanated Heaven (Anu) as his primary manifestation, to mirror his existence to the world.

Professor Parpola rightly points out that this comes very close to Kabbalistic metaphysics.

He believes that the pattern continues thus:

- (3) Sin is Ea (60) divided by 2 = 30.
- (4) Marduk is Ea (60) – Sin (30 divided by 3) = 50.
- (5) Shamash is (Ea or 60 divided by 3) = 20.
- (6) Ishtar is (Ea or 60 divided by 4) = 15.
- (7) Nabu is 60 – (60 divided by 3) (or 2 times 20) = 40.
- (8) Adad is 60 divided by 6 =10.
- (9) Nergal is Ishtar or 15 – 1 (or 2 times 7) = 14.

There are so many layers of meaning to peel away that it is like an onion. There are no books from Assyria to explain all this. The diagrams had to be interpreted orally by scholars to apprentice students. There was an oral tradition of spiritual teaching, exactly as in the later Kabbalah, which is the main reason that dating is so controversial in that field. When you recall that the Greek bards had to learn by heart the entire Iliad and Odyssey of Homer, and they succeeded in doing so, it is obvious that huge amounts of learning were and are capable of being carried in people's heads. We must not underestimate its volume. It is a commonplace (but one of doubtful accuracy) that we normally use only about 1/10 of our brain capacity. The memories of professional stage actors and actresses are truly impressive.

Key points
- Temples were measured by sacred numbers of the god to which they were dedicated; this practice was originated by the Assyrians in the 13th century BC and copied by the Greeks
- The Tree of Life has 10 sephiroth, which means numbers or countings, exactly as if counted on 10 digits
- Assyrian gods are placed on the sephiroth by number and

epithet; the epithets correspond exactly to the Hebrew names of the sephiroth

- Arithmetic shows that the number of the whole Tree is 360, the key number in Mesopotamia
- The negative pillar has numbers to subtract from those on the positive pillar
- Ishtar is at Tiphereth in the heart of the Tree; all other attributions are to gods
- The state god Ashur corresponds to the Ain Soph Aur; it is above the Tree but not on it
- The triadic structure of the Tree is linked to the typical triadic pattern of Semitic gods
- The Tree is also a Family Tree, working downwards
- The story of creation is a mathematical code

Chapter 3

All Ways Lead to the Goddess

One of the most interesting aspects of the attribution of gods to the sephiroth is that Ishtar is in the centre. There she sits in the prime position, surrounded by male gods, in this glyph from the region strongly associated with patriarchal religions. This begs for an explanation; and scholars of the Kabbalah may want to relate this feminine aspect to the later concept of the Shekhinah, which is about as close as Judaism comes to the Christian concept of the Holy Spirit or Holy Ghost.[29]

I asked myself, was there a "tree and goddess" correlation in Mesopotamia which I had missed and, if so, would it help to make sense of this arrangement? I found that, as I turned to Sumerian materials available in translation, there was exactly the missing jigsaw piece that I describe.

The Sumerian precursor of Ishtar was Inanna[30]. She seems to have had a more broad and peaceful definition than Ishtar. She was a triple goddess of heaven, earth and the underworld; this in itself put me in mind of the middle pillar with its various stages. Ishtar with her aspect of love and war goddess seems to have a more narrow focus; she relates to the affairs of the earth rather than heaven or the underworld. So that would explain why Ishtar is related to the middle sephirah of the middle pillar.

There is a good deal of Sumerian literature available in translation about Inanna. I found a poem concerning Inanna and the Huluppu Tree. This has many elements in embryo of the Garden of Eden story – a tree, a man, a woman, a sexual temptress (the demoness Lilith), a snake in the roots, and a river mentioned in the Genesis story itself.

I was not at first able to tell what type or species of tree is this Huluppu tree but it was just as mysterious as that tree in the

Bible. Some have guessed at the willow, but others say the date-palm, which is the most commonly found tree in this region's art. Inanna was called, "Lady of the Date Clusters," according to Thorkild Jacobsen. The fruits of the date apparently correspond to Dumuzi, the male lover of Inanna, and he was called, "The one great source of the date clusters". If Eve offered date fruits to

Adam, he must have eaten a date rather than an apple. My question was not finally answered until I came across the Norton Critical Edition of the Epic of Gilgamesh, translated and edited by Benjamin R. Foster and published in 2001. At p.129 this whole story of the Huluppu Tree reappears as part of the story of Gilgamesh and the tree is definitely identified there as a poplar. While I have no wish to challenge the accuracy of that translation, I note that this is one text only and there remains the possibility that other ancient textual versions of the story referred to other types of tree, just as the Assyrian palace reliefs clearly have more than one species of sacred tree; the religious iconography of Inanna and Ishtar makes it likely, in my opinion, that some versions of the text may have referred to the date-palm tree.

In both versions it is clear that Inanna expected to have various items, namely a throne and a bed, carved out of its trunk. These are both resting places, where she was stationed. The throne of Ishtar would be at Tiphereth on the Kabbalistic Tree. The man who eventually carved these items was Gilgamesh, King of Uruk, a distant relation, although called brother in the poem. Uruk (or Erech) is an ancient city in the south of the country which gave its name to modern Iraq.

If the date palm is the main Tree of Life commonly shown on the Assyrian palace reliefs, this could neatly explain the lattice-work pattern that is so evident. The trunk of the commonly seen variety of palm tree is patterned in that way because it grows upwards with new leaves, which leave the lattice pattern when they fall off. Another possibility is that branches of trees were deliberately tied together at the nodes and fashioned into a lattice; or living branches were trained in those directions as an *espalier*.

One theory of the genies that protect the tree is that they are not holding pine cones at all but rather they have the male flower of the date and are pollinating the tree, while holding a bucket of male flowers, so that it will continue to bear dates in the following year. This is a very attractive theory because the date palm was a great source of food and the date-palm is emblematic of the region[31].

Some of the abstract trees shown in Assyrian art are clearly pomegranates, as the fruit is distinctive, but many others are much more like date-palms. Parpola notes that this artistic form of the Tree is principally characterized by the "garland" of cones, pomegranates, or palmettes surrounding its crown and/or trunk. I suggest that the pomegranates designate that species and the palmettes designate a palm tree.

Inanna was later to become a confident Queen but here she has not yet obtained her throne, so her character is that of an adolescent, hoping for a hero to save the day, not yet fully aware of adult life but clear on what she needs in order to live it. We all go through a stage of leaving our parents' home and acquiring our first furniture; here this all has Royal connotations.

The mention of a snake in the roots of the tree put me in mind once again of yogic teachings about kundalini. A summary of the relevant points will be found in appendix one. It may also be relevant that the Sumerian tale of Inanna's Descent into the Underworld contains an account of the transformation of her husband Dumuzi into a snake by Utu, the Sumerian sun god. This snake-disguise allowed Dumuzi to escape from the demons of the underworld. Dumuzi represented the enduring cyclical fertility of nature which was restored every autumn as the hot summer ended. I can picture in my mind's eye Sumerian children at the end of a long, hot summer spying a snake and shouting excitedly, "There's Dumuzi!"

The historical Dumuzi[32] ruled Uruk immediately before Gilgamesh, according to the Sumerian King list[33]. This period has been dated to approximately 2500-2275 BC.

There are plenty of trees to choose from, if you want to find a tree of life or a *Huluppu* tree. Trees like tamarisk, acacia, terebinth, sycamore, poplar and willow were used for fuel, the manufacture of tools, furniture and household implements, and the construction of small buildings. A variety of trees also supplied resins and medicinal ointments. Also, nut-trees (almond and pistachio) and fruit-trees (fig, pomegranate and date) were important sources of food. The olive tree provided oil that had a multitude of uses. Evergreens from the high mountains, such as cedars of Lebanon, were highly prized for ship-building. There are many books which explain the variety and uses of trees in this period.[34]

Professor Parpola further explains that Assyrian texts frequently speak of "the gods and Ishtar," the singular implying that there was, in fact, only one, not several, "female deities". He says such a course "perfectly agrees with the Tree diagram, where Ishtar is surrounded by eight male deities; compare the Kabbalistic parable in *Bahir* explaining the "divine fullness" as a garden planted with nine male (palm) trees and one feminine tree (the ethrog), analyzed in Scholem, *Origins of the Kabbalah*, p.172[35]. (The *ethrog* is a bright yellow citrus fruit, resembling a lumpy lemon, which grows in the Eastern Mediterranean and is used in the Jewish Feast of *Succoth*.) He also notes that the term *ilani* "gods" has a well known equivalent in the Hebrew *elohim* which is also plural. (The Near East had a concept of the Council of Gods and it seems that the Hebrew deity in the early conception may have had a role as speaker or messenger in this Council, which would explain why the deity of the Old Testament was so strongly associated with prophecy and communication.)

The hero of the story of the *Huluppu* tree is Gilgamesh, a legendary strong man, King of Uruk. His action gives the tale a happy ending. He supports Inanna here and they both benefit thereby. This outcome contrasts with the conflict and unhappy ending of both the Garden of Eden story and also of Gilgamesh's encounter with Inanna's successor, Ishtar, in the *Epic of*

Gilgamesh.

Lilith has become the focus of much modern interest and some misunderstandings have arisen. It is clear to me that she was not a goddess but a demoness[36], who preyed on babies and tempted men – the married woman's worst nightmare. I suspect that the well-known artwork depicting a clawed, winged Lilith was intended to appease or repel her, rather than to attract her malign attention. She has aspects of the vampire and the succubus and may have been blamed for cot deaths. She is not connected with any Egyptian Goddess and certainly not with Isis, as I have heard it said. In fact, if Ishtar is connected with a throne, then it would be Ishtar, not Lilith, who can be correlated with Isis. The throne of the Egyptian Pharaoh was personified and called Aset. The Greek form of that name, Isis, became popular in Egypt at a much later date (after the conquest of Alexander in the 4th century BC). Wings are routinely attributed in Mesopotamian art to both "good" and "bad" supernatural beings. Care needs to be taken not to confuse demons with angels.

Here is a translation of relevant parts of the poem *"The Huluppu Tree"*, taken from "Inanna, Queen of Heaven and Earth" by Diane Wolkstein and Samuel Noah Kramer[37]:

"…..In the first days…
……When heaven had moved away from earth,
And earth had separated from heaven,
And the name of man was fixed;
When the Sky God, An, had carried off the heavens,
And the Air God, Enlil, had carried off the earth,
…..
At that time, a tree, a single tree, a *Huluppu* tree
Was planted by the banks of the Euphrates.
The tree was nurtured by the waters of the Euphrates.
The whirling South Wind arose, pulling at its roots
And ripping at its branches

Until the waters of the Euphrates carried it away.

A woman ......
Plucked the tree from the river and spoke:

"I shall bring this tree to Uruk.
I shall plant this tree in my holy garden."

Inanna cared for the tree with her hand.
She settled the earth around the tree with her foot.
She wondered:

"How long will it be until I have a shining throne to sit upon?
How long will it be until I have a shining bed to lie upon?"

The years passed; five years, then ten years.
The tree grew thick,
But its bark did not split.
Then a serpent who could not be charmed
Made its nest in the roots of the *Huluppu* tree.
The *Anzu* bird set his young in the branches of the trunk.
The young woman who loved to laugh wept.
How Inanna wept!
(Yet they would not leave her tree.)

.......Inanna called to her brother Gilgamesh..."

[Gilgamesh fixed her problem as he is usually a hero in Mesopotamian literature. There are artistic scenes of him displayed at the British Museum and elsewhere. The *Anzu*-bird is thought to be a lion-headed thunder-bird.]

If the theories are right (1) that Inanna/Ishtar is the goddess personified at the heart of the Tree and (2) that the Tree is a date palm, then I may have an explanation for the rather extraordinary representations of the goddess Diana of the Ephesians, well known both from the New Testament and from archaeology. I recently visited the Sir John Soane Museum in Lincoln's Inn. Sir John was an inveterate collector of large classical artefacts, dug up on the Great Tour of continental Europe and the Near East. I turned a corner and suddenly came face to face with Diana of the Ephesians. She stands straight with her legs together, very tree-like, and instead of two breasts she has a chest covered with dozens of bulbous shapes which have puzzled scholars for a long time. Some have assumed they were breasts but there is nothing

in nature which has nearly so many. Below them, on her trunk and legs, there are rows of birds, beasts and insects, including stags and bees. This Diana is not the fierce wandering huntress under the pale inconstant moon, known as Artemis, worshipped by the Greeks. She is instead a manifestation of the Mother Earth, and I am in favour of interpreting the bulbous shapes as dates. She resembles to me a personified date-palm or Tree spirit. The palm tree is emblematic of the Near East. The bees represent the process of fertilization as they spread pollen between flowers. If we imagine an oasis in the desert, surrounded by palm trees shading many cool beasts, birds and insects, then we may see more clearly what is meant by the archetypal Tree of Life and so reinstate the proper context for this Diana.

The date-palm has been grown in North Africa for more than 8,000 years and is used, for example, in construction work[38]. It is a source of food and shade and was thus essential to the development of civilization in the Near East. The fruit has over 300 known medicinal uses, and its fruit is implicated in low rates of cancer and heart disease (according to recent studies of Bedouin Arabs who eat dates on a daily basis). Up to 200 dates can grow in one cluster. This is one compelling reason why I suspect that the bulbous shapes on Diana are dates rather than breasts. The ancient Egyptians used the leaf to represent longevity (a direct link to the Tree of Life concept) and the strewing of palm leaves before Jesus, commemorated in the Christian Feast of Palm Sunday, should be seen against this background. In the Muslim Holy Month of Ramadan, Muslims break their fast with dates.

An individual palm tree is either male or female. Left to its own devices, the tree may never grow tall enough to produce fruit. The male is non-productive, apart from its vital role in pollination. Mankind has pollinated them manually in cultivated palm tree groves, to ensure high food production rates. I now believe that this is the most likely explanation of the winged genies with buckets, shown in Assyrian palace art.

The cultivated groves known from ancient Mesopotamia onwards have just a few male trees so that the female trees can produce many dates. An acre of date trees averages one male to forty-nine female trees. The male blossom is fluffy, white and star-shaped, while the female resembles beads on a string. The dates are ready for harvesting about 7 months after pollination. The female date is considered holy and bears the fruit. The goddess Inanna (the Sumerian ancestor of the Roman love goddess, Venus) was known as "the one who makes the dates full of abundance".

Date-palm seeds have been found in the ancient Jewish fortress of Masada, which was besieged by the Romans, ending with a mass suicide in 73 AD. One of these seeds has been germinated in 2005, by Dr Elaine Solowey, and thus became the oldest seed ever brought back to life[39]. This experiment has revived an extinct Judaean palm, exactly like the fictional recreation of dinosaurs in *Jurassic Park*. The date-palms normally grown in modern Israel were imported from California, derived from a strain originating in Iraq. Native Judaean palms were destroyed by the Crusaders, as they gave nourishment to their opponents. In Roman times, forests of succulent date-palms had covered the area from Lake Galilee to the Dead Sea. The Biblical description of Canaan as a "land flowing with milk and honey" refers to date honey, not bees' honey, because those palm trees were very widespread at the time. Any references in the Bible to Sacred Trees (whether pagan or Jewish) are therefore likely to have had the date-palm in the writer's mind.

Key points

- Ishtar was the Semitic form of Sumerian Inanna, an earlier "Venus" goddess
- Inanna is connected in legend to a tree
- The *huluppu* tree story connects many elements which recur in the Garden of Eden story from Genesis
- The hero is strong-man Gilgamesh, King of Uruk
- Inanna has a connection with the middle of the tree, like Ishtar
- Unlike the Genesis story, this has a happy ending
- Inanna may be the origin of Diana of the Ephesians, as a personified date-palm
- The cultivated date palm is the common link between the fertility religion of Inanna and the genies with buckets

Chapter 4

Venus Has A Long History

One of the strongest correlations in Kabbalah is the persistent attribution of planets to particular sephiroth. This is not surprising, if the Kabbalah originates in Mesopotamia, because the ancient Mesopotamians worshipped planetary gods in their religion. In modern Kabbalah, the planet Venus is attributed to the sephirah *Netzach* but the Assyrians attributed it to the central sephirah *Tiphereth*. The Venus tradition is extremely old. In ancient societies, Venus was observed by astronomers who left records and also in fact their observation points. It seems that Venus was regarded as the most important of the planets, which is not surprising because she is the brightest of them.

Venus[40], as the goddess of love and fertile date-palms adored in Mesopotamia under names such as Ishtar and Inanna, is derived from Venus the planet. The planet does something very peculiar in the heavens. It is the only planet which appears to move in a regular geometric pattern, which happens to be a pentagram. (Obviously its *real* motion around the sun is a squashed circle or ellipse but I am describing here its *apparent* motion seen from earth.) This has been noticed for as long as there have been astronomers.

The modern flag of Morocco bears a five-pointed star, not the crescent moon one might expect. The Turkish flag design includes a five-pointed star. The five pointed star or pentagram was known as a symbol of good luck in the Near East for thousands of years before Christ. (As a stick-figure, it is the fairly common Egyptian hieroglyph *seba* for "star" but this may not be the direct origin of the geometric figure.) It was copied by the Greeks, whose vases show it as a symbol in a shield and found its way into medieval literature as the heraldic motif of the

Knight, Sir Gawain, in *Sir Gawain and the Green Knight* – a story which involves entry into a mysterious prehistoric tumulus described as "The Green Chapel". (This explanation of the Green Chapel was put to me by Geoff and/or Fran Doel in their excellent and memorable course on Arthurian Literature held at Westonbirt, near Tetbury, Gloucestershire, in 1991, and now adapted into book form as *Worlds of Arthur* by Doel, Doel & Lloyd (Tempus).) It also occurred to me that the story (probably written by a well-read and mischievous monk) might even contain elements of ancient knowledge about Venus , starting as it does from a challenge issued at the winter solstice, the significance of which I will explain shortly. (Geoffrey Chaucer was also using planetary themes in his writings.)

According to Christopher Knight and Robert Lomas, writing in *Uriel's Machine: The Ancient Origins of Science* at p.464: "The five-pointed star...is certainly a representation of Venus' movements around the sun as viewed from Earth. The Grooved Ware People knew that an understanding of the forty year cycle of Venus, through five of these five-pointed star cycles, was a perfect calendar/clock. In fact, until atomic clocks were invented a few years ago, there was no more accurate means of checking the passage of time than studying the position of Venus against the backdrop of the stars."

What I have not stated is that they are talking about the ceiling of an English Masonic temple, which I have never seen, since I have never been a Mason. They attempted to persuade their readers that there were some very ancient beliefs encoded within Masonry. I note that there are thousands of years to account for in this Masonic part of their theory.

They contend that the Grooved Ware People (named after the grooves on their pottery) lived in Western Europe until 2655 BC. These people built a complex of temples which were carefully engineered to allow the light of Venus to shine into dark chambers just before sunrise, or just after sunset, once every eight years. Their structures include Newgrange, Knowth and Dowth in Ireland's Boyne Valley; the rings of Brodgar and Stenness, Maes Howe and Callanish in the north of Scotland; Barclodiad Y Gawres and Bryn Celli Ddu (pronounced Brin Kethli Thee) in north-west Wales; and Stonehenge, Avebury, Silbury Hill and Durrington Walls in the south of England.

Note that these centers of science are located, roughly speaking, in each of the modern countries that make up the islands of Britain and Ireland: you have centres for England, Wales, Scotland and Ireland. This may tell us that administration naturally falls into a repeating pattern. Presumably at this time we are looking at tribal confederacies. It is difficult to name them because the Roman era literature which does name the tribes is much later and changes quite a lot even in that short period.

Are some of these structures, not the rings or henges but the subterranean structures, real life "Green Chapels" as described in the Gawain story? I have visited those listed in Wales and England and can see a striking resemblance. One comparison that comes to mind is the charnel house at Avebury known as the West Kennet Long Barrow. This is at the top of a sloping field and is indeed very long. Inside it is like a filing cabinet for the specially tended parts of ancestral skeletons, now long gone: lots of separate compartments run off a main corridor. We are here in a world of shamanic spirits who, like the Green Giant in the Gawain story, may have talked to our ancestors.

These people invented the megalithic yard and built hundreds of stone circles to act as "horizon declinometers", providing accurate calendars. Many of the apparent carvings, which have been acclaimed as possible early writing, link the separate areas: particularly the "spiral and lozenge" motif found on the Skara Brae potsherds, which appear on stones at Newgrange and at Barclodiad Y Gawres, as well as at locations on the Iberian Peninsula.

The dating of the disappearance of the Grooved Ware People

from Europe coincides with the building of the first pyramid at Saqqara in Egypt and the first ziggurat in Iraq. Astronomical cultures throughout the Near East had a major impetus for very mysterious reasons at the same time as the megalith builders mysteriously stopped.

Knight and Lomas are clearly excited by the likelihood that there was a migration of an advanced astronomical culture to the Near East, with a science based on observations of Venus. In other words, Venus was at the heart of their science, just as Venus (as Ishtar) is at the heart of the Assyrian Tree of Life, a concept which seems to come to Assyria from Sumer where the ziggurats were first built and Inanna (Ishtar's precursor) was the prime goddess. And the earliest astrological text that survives is on display in the British Museum, known as The Venus Tablet of King Amisaduqa of Babylon; it records the appearances and disappearances of Venus in the hope of deriving omens from them. Venus was a particular favourite of the Mesopotamian astronomers/astrologers and was part of the Holy Trinity of the Assyrio-Babylonian civilization, along with the Sun and moon. And that culture was so interested in measuring that we still use their units of measure today.

I will examine the timeline more closely. In 1998 the oldest known stone circle observatory was discovered, at Nabta, west of Abu Simbel in the desert of Southernmost Egypt[41]. This was erected around 6500 years ago, more than 2000 years before Stonehenge. The stones are 9 feet high and are proof of a basic knowledge of the stars and sun, being aligned, it is thought, with the summer solstice, so that no shadow is cast then. I believe this does not detract from the Knight & Lomas argument, which deals with a later period.

I turn now to events which were scrutinized by Knight & Lomas. A lot happens in about 2700 BC. Silbury Hill is built, still for mysterious reasons (possibly astronomical) as it is clearly not a tomb, near Avebury in Wiltshire. At the same time bronze artefacts exist in Wiltshire. The first ziggurat is built in Iraq (for astronomer-priests, in all likelihood) and the Old Kingdom of Egypt ends (which is a major trauma for Egypt). The first known royal inscription of the Sumerians is found, that of the King of Kish. Kish dominated Sumer (in the south of Mesopotamia) until about 2400 BC, when King Sargon of Akkad (in the north) built the first great Mesopotamian Empire. The two kingdoms of north and south were thus united, rather as the Egyptian states had been earlier.

In 2655 BC Skara Brae is abandoned, for mysterious reasons. In 2650 BC the First Pyramid is built at Saqqara, Egypt and the reign of Gilgamesh ends in Uruk, Sumer/Babylonia (you will recall he is a character in the *Huluppu Tree* story). In 2638 BC Khufu or Cheops becomes King of the Two Lands of Egypt and he leaves the Great Pyramid as his lasting memorial. The ancient Egyptian pyramids that covered the Giza plateau were covered in pieces of quartz; as Knight & Lomas noted with great interest: *in size and dressed (levelled) front section, these pieces of quartz were identical to the Newgrange stones.*

In 2500 BC the Avebury stones are set up (in a circle much larger than Stonehenge) and megalithic building stops in Orkney.

The overall impression these events leave is of decay in the north-west and an astonishing and very rapid resurgence in the south-east, possibly involving some migration of high level expertise, a "brain drain" in modern parlance. We may be looking at the effect of a migration of a social class of people rather than an invasion of the entire community, and certainly many people already lived in Egypt and Mesopotamia, for thousands of years, at the very least, before 2700 BC.

The Grooved Ware People abandoned their Orkney base and their observatories fell into disuse. Their burial practices were replaced by those of the *physically different* Beaker people. The newcomer Beaker people had round skulls whereas the Grooved

Ware People had elongated skulls. I am being careful not to suggest that there was a complete emptying of the land followed by a mass migration without any intermarriage. The evidence simply suggests that the newcomers outnumbered the indigenous population when they moved in and that there was a cultural hiatus. It was certainly difficult to sustain populations on the islands off Scotland and if times were hard you would expect them to be abandoned; but it might have been a different story on the mainland.

These ancient astronomers (we might think of them - no doubt anachronistically - as "techno-druids") engineered Newgrange in Ireland to address the midwinter sunrise. This is now commonly accepted. At Maes Howe, Knight and Lomas tell (at p.495) how Venus lights the chamber twice in the afternoon on the winter solstice. Every eight years Venus causes a double flash of light into the chamber at Maes Howe. The name means "the field of the evening after the sun has set", if the Pictish is similar to the Welsh term, "Maes Hwyr". (I already knew that Pictish was related to Welsh and had been replaced relatively recently by Gaelic and then English, as Pictish Ogham inscriptions exist in Scotland and are presumably of similar date to the Welsh and Irish Ogham stone inscriptions.) This Venus phenomenon happened in 1996 and 2004; it will repeat at 8 year intervals through 2012, 2020 and so on. The double alignment of the solar solstice and Venus could hardly be accidental.

Similarly, at Bryn Celli Ddu, Knight and Lomas conclude (p.266) that there is evidence that the chamber was designed for a very small number of people to enter and observe the solar and Venus cycles with great accuracy. Their reasoning is that every eight years it marks a point when the solar calendar, the lunar calendar and the sidereal (position of the stars) calendar all coincide to within a few minutes. Over forty years, five such cycles, it synchronizes these calendars to within a few seconds. The eight year Venus cycle also accurately maps the moon's phases and its sidereal movements to within five hours. The practical benefits include detailed forecasting of both tides and lunar eclipses.

Thousands of years later, a new astrological religion called Mithraism (see appendix two) was to sweep across Europe, involving star-worship in a cave or underground chamber, representing *the cosmos from inside*. Its initiatory grades were linked to the planets. It has left no holy book behind. Was this simply the latest form of the ancient religion of the megalithic chambers, the "Green Chapels"?

Key points

- The five-pointed star or pentagram is an ancient symbol of Venus (and no other planet) for astronomical reasons
- The pentagram is an ancient symbol of good luck
- From Ancient Greek times, it was used as a heraldic symbol by armed knights
- The story of Gawain and the Green Knight takes elements from the megalithic Venus cult
- The megalithic Venus cult had observatories targeted on Venus at the Winter Solstice
- The megalithic astronomers appear to have migrated around 2700 BC from Western Europe to the Near East and were involved with the development of stepped observatories
- Early writing may also show a parallel motion, starting with rock symbols

Chapter 5

Gilgamesh And Ascension Up The Tree

The Assyrian Tree is a map of a journey. If you unfold the path of the Lightning Flash (the vertical zigzag sequence joining the *sephiroth* used by the Kabbalists) but keep the same sequence of god names, you have the Mystic Path which the hero Gilgamesh passes along in the Epic. The story is arranged in twelve tablets, divided into four levels. Professor Parpola has again produced a helpful diagram.

There are 12 Tablets here. Tablet 12 refers to Sephirah 1, Tablet 11 to Sephirah 2, Tablet 10 to Sephirah 3 and so on down to the base of the Tree.

Gilgamesh is a solar hero, of divine ancestry, a precursor of Hercules and Samson. Hercules has 12 Labours which relate to the signs of the zodiac. Gilgamesh also had astral events in his legends. For example, he deals with scorpion men (Scorpio) and

The Via Mystica in the Gilgamesh Epic

LEVEL	GOD	TABLET	STATE
Isle of Saints: Outside ordinary time and space	Anu	XII	Union with God, Eternal Life
"	Ea	XI	The Ultimate Wisdom, Accepting God's Will
"	Sin	X	Understanding Man's fate and the purpose of life
Refining a purified soul	Mummu	IX	Altered states, Contact with the Divine, Glimpse of Paradise
"	Marduk, Enlil	VIII	Practice of magnanimity compassion and mercy
"	Shamash	VII	Exposures to the trials and severities of life
Learning to know oneself	Ishtar	VI	Withstanding major temptations
"	Nabu, Ninurta	V	Victory over the ego
"	Adad, Girru, Nusku	IV	Practice of honesty and virtues, love of neighbour, hope
The animal man	-	III	Discovery of the Path
"	-	II	Awakening of consciousness, sorrow over one's condition, desire for change
"	Nergal, Sakkan	I	Bestiality and animal instincts, selfishness and greed

the bull of heaven (Taurus) sent by Ishtar and her father the Sun god Shamash. In astrology Venus is said to rule the sign of the bull.

It is well known that Gilgamesh sought immortality. He was told he could obtain immortality from the flower of a prickly plant which grew underwater far away. He did find the plant and took hold of the flower but a serpent which lived in the water snatched the flower away from him and so he lost it.

The best known scene in the Epic is probably his dispute with Ishtar. (See Tablet 6 and sephirah 6.) A family friend, Claire Wall, from Fresno, California, pointed out to me that Gilgamesh made a mistake with Ishtar, and instead of refusing her bed and name-calling, he should have slept with her and become uplifted by her divinity. This would have paralleled the civilising of his friend the wild man Enkidu by the prostitute, with whom Enkidu lay for 7 days. His rejection of Ishtar leads to the fight with the Bull of Heaven. In ancient myth, lovemaking and fertility is linked to life, so a rejection of lovemaking is a rejection of the natural order. As Gilgamesh is a King, he is in the same position as the legendary Fisher King, whose sexual function relates directly to the fertility of the land. Kings are supposed to produce heirs and that doesn't happen if they reject the Goddess of Love.

Gilgamesh could have appeased Ishtar by accepting her generous offer. Basically she had the power to destroy him anyway so he was at risk whatever he did with her. He could have gone to her temple, prayed, used her name as a mantra, burnt incense, made other offerings and so on. The emphasis in their religion was on appeasing angry gods, due to a fear of retribution if they were angered. The whole culture's stability rested on the assumption that kings would protect the people by appeasing the gods. This is the bargain behind the divine right of kings. In political terms, if you had a powerful priesthood or priesshood, you had to get on with them. This was the norm in Mesopotamia and Egypt (but not the Indus Valley).

The fight with Ishtar is in the 6th tablet of the Epic and Parpola considers that it relates to the withstanding of major temptations. But the question remains, was the temptation to bed Ishtar - or in fact - not to bed Ishtar?

Parpola also relates this Path to the Mesopotamian Myth of Etana. The central motif is a man's ascent to heaven on an eagle's back. It has been classed as an adventure story or early sci-fi. The eagle inhabits a tree which is Etana himself and so does a serpent. Etana finds the eagle on a mountain where he feeds it and teaches it to fly again. An allegory of spiritual training and self-discipline. Eventually he reaches a celestial *ekallu* or palace. This is very reminiscent of the ascent motif in the *Hekhaloth* texts (more or less the same word, in fact) and later mystical literature dealing with the riders of the chariot. The heavenward ascent of Etana is already attested on the seals from 2300 BCE, thousands of years before any surviving Qabalistic texts. It was of course an oral tradition first.

I will shortly move on to discuss Babylon and commence the astrological part of this book. If the Assyrian Tree shows the connection between Heaven and Earth – "As above so below" – then we need to examine what was the Babylonian view of Heaven. I will finish this section by recapping on those genies and the Tree.

Doorways and gateways could let in evil so they needed protection. This tradition of protecting an entrance door has been maintained by the Jewish people. The British traditionally do it with horseshoes. The genies are sometimes winged bulls. The Assyrians lived in a permanent Astrological Age of Taurus the Bull, as nobody had discovered the Precession of the Equinoxes. The bulls were protected by winged djinn or genies. Mostly genies or guardian angels are shown with bird wings and often with bird heads. This is the origin of winged angels in the Judeo-Christian tradition and in Qabalah of course. The pine cone sprinklers were possibly used for holy water, as a blessing on the Tree and the King, which are the same. Some portraits feature a winged god (probably Ashur rather than Shamash) overhead in a chariot, in the same position as Ain Soph Aur. And he appears in battle fighting on the Assyrian side. Good luck was his to bestow.

Key points

- The 12 tablets of the Epic of Gilgamesh relate to ascension up the Tree via the sephiroth on a spiritual journey (like "Pilgrim's Progress")
- The conflict with Ishtar may have been a mistake
- Gilgamesh is a strong "solar hero" like Hercules and Samson
- The ascension myth of Etana is a forerunner of early Kabbalistic Hekhaloth texts, dealing with "riders of the chariot" to celestial palaces
- The genies are early "guardian angels" who protect the Tree/King and start the whole angel tradition
- The Assyrian King is a manifestation of the divine Tree of Life

Part 2

South:

The Stars Above

Chapter 6

Divination Gives Birth to Astrology[42]

My main source for Chapters 6 and 7 is Michael Baigent's "From The Omens of Babylon" (Arkana, 1994, 1st edition) and I am extremely grateful to him for permission to use his material. It supplies a key step in my argument, which would have taken me far longer to assemble in any other way, if it were even possible. A much briefer and less contemporary introduction to the subject is found at Chapter 11 of Rupert Gleadow's "The Origin of the Zodiac", first published in 1968 and also by C B F Walker in Chapter 1 of History & Astrology edited by Annabella Kitson (Mandala,1989). In 2008 Continuum published "A History of Western Astrology Vol.1 " by Dr Nicholas Campion.

Astrology seems to have started in Sumer and continued in Babylon and spread out, eventually resulting in a huge library collection in Nineveh (Mosul) during the Assyrian period. We have seen how King Gudea of Lagash in Sumer was instructed by gods in a dream to build a temple according to the stars. The Epic of Gilgamesh, dating from the 3rd millennium BC, tells the story of the hero-king of Uruk. This precursor of the tale of Hercules and the Twelve Labours (which relates to the zodiac) has some star references to zodiacal creatures such as the Bull of Heaven, the Lions and the Scorpion-Men. The equinoxes were important; in Sumer the New Year festival was held at the Autumn Equinox, with rites to Inanna and Dumuzi, whereas in Babylon the rites involved Marduk and other gods and were held at the Spring Equinox.

Astrology grew out of a broader obsession with omens in general[43]. The reason that these people loved omens is that they were very scared of demons, ghosts and bad luck in general. If you have seen horror movies such as *The Exorcist* or *Wishmaster*, you will recognize the Demonic form of Pazuzu, the four-winged, beast-headed demon that was most feared in these lands. The sinister four wings recall insects, perhaps plagues of locusts that brought starvation. These images of Pazuzu were used not to attract evil, by sympathetic magic, but to turn it away, by apotropaic magic, from the Greek *trope* turn, *apo* away. He appeared on amulets worn by pregnant women. Many kinds of omens were read in order to foretell evil and create opportunities for favourable intervention by magic. Fate could be changed by magic. Oil dropped in water created patterns that could be read in trance, remarkably similar to the shapes in the 1960s "lava lamp". Birds, entrails and so on were employed. The face of Humbaba, a demon defeated by Gilgamesh, may be an interpreter's map of the intestines.

The liver was the favourite organ. Taken from a sacrificed animal such as a ram, blemishes would be sought by a baru priest and then compared with a chart of sectors to identify the precise meaning. There was a scientific endeavour behind all this but the relation of cause and effect was seen differently from today. This haruspication or augury was passed on by the baru priests to Asia Minor where the forebears of the Etruscans lived. They emigrated to Tuscany in Northern Italy and passed the techniques to the Romans. Cicero was a member of the College of Augurs. In time astrology, which did not involve the loss of expensive animals, was to supercede augury.

Omens from the stars were collected by the tupsharru priests for the King. They did not do personal astrology, just omens for the King and State, mundane or political astrology. They looked at the sun, moon and stars in the heavens. They had stepped towers or ziggurats (Babylonian pyramids) which could provide them with observation platforms although that was probably not their original purpose. In their rituals they would face the four quarters looking for stars linked to the equinoxes and solstices and then make symbolic gestures in the air to invoke their protection (possibly in the form of pentagrams). My under-standing is that the stars in question[44] were Aldebaran in Taurus (Spring Equinox), Regulus in Leo (Summer Solstice), Antares in Scorpio (Autumn Equinox) and Fomalhaut in Pisces (Winter Solstice). Those were in the Persian tradition[45] the Royal Watchers or Guardians of the Sky. These priests were taught by the father in their family and were expected to be successful. If their star forecasts were wrong they could lose their living as court astrologer. So they tended to hedge their bets and they scrutinized the heavens very carefully. They worked in teams through the night.

The earliest astrological record surviving is the Venus Tablet of the Babylonian King Amisaduqa who reigned about 1600 BCE. These were observations of the appearance and disappearance of Venus from the night sky. It can disappear for months at a time. The gaps were hoped to have value for forecasting. This data was in use for at least 7 centuries as the tablet shown here is a late copy from about 1000 BCE. Venus was the most important of the true planets and in fact is the closest to earth of them all and therefore the brightest.

The earliest astrology, from c.2000 BC onwards, had no zodiac, rising signs, houses or degrees. Instead they considered the planets in relation to the horizon. The eastern horizon was divided into gates or palaces of three gods, which is quite different from placing the planets in the zodiac band or ecliptic. A planet was observed in the path or gate of Anu, Enlil, or Ea, all of which fell on the eastern horizon. In effect, this was a rough and ready assessment of relative celestial latitude. The zodiac first appeared as 18 irregular constellations and only later became 12 equal signs of 30 degrees.

Characteristics of the Babylonian Gods were incorporated into astrological interpretation and have remained largely unchanged in modern practice. By the start of the Common Era we had personal horoscopes, rising signs, houses and many aspects between planets recorded in degrees of arc. It was Berossus, a Babylonian priest who brought astrology west to the island of Cos where it was taken up by Greek philosophers such as Plato and the Stoics.

Each planet related to a god, so the Sun was Shamash, Moon was Sin, Mercury was Nabu, Venus was Ishtar, Mars was Nergal, Jupiter was Marduk and Saturn was Ninurta. I cannot emphasise enough that Sin[46] was generally seen as male and the chief god. Male moon deities were commonplace in the Near East in contrast to Europe. The Sinai Peninsula was named after him and he had major cult centres at Harran and Ur. He was seen as a wise old man with a beard. The moon was Lord of the Night Sky and used for measurement which was difficult with the other heavenly bodies.

Eclipses - where the sun or moon were hidden from observers on Earth - were the most important omen to predict and they were bad news for the King. Action had to be taken first. The King needed rituals to be performed. Sometimes a substitute king was put on the throne for 100 days and then "sent to his destiny". He could not talk or give orders so there was no danger of him usurping any power. Other rituals involving exorcisms, incense, prayer, chanting etc were also carried out and the whole package was classed as Namburbi rituals[47]. We don't know why these individuals were picked on or what benefit they received for being substitutes. Namburbi rituals with substitutes were performed as late as the 3rd century BC.

Boundary stones or *kudurru* were land markers, title deeds showing ownership. Written in stone they were meant to last for eternity. They could not be forged as divine powers were invoked. These included the holy trinity of Moon, Sun and Venus.

The Assyrian kings also liked the protection of these gods. The symbols on their stelae may be interpreted thus. The moon Sin is the crescent; the sun Shamash or Bel is often connected by scholars with the equal armed cross or winged circle figure; Venus is a star, often with 7 or 8 rays; the forked tongs are the storm god Hadad and presumably represent his lightning flash; the horned helmet is either Ashur or Enlil. (If the winged disc is Shamash, then the choice is open but if the winged disc is Ashur, the horned helmet must by elimination be Enlil.) Jeremy Black, University Lecturer in Akkadian at Oxford, writes that, astronomically, Enlil was associated with the constellation Bootes[48]; and in Neo-Assyrian art (i.e. after c.930 BC), Enlil is symbolized by a horned cap. The various titles of Enlil include Great Mountain, King of the Foreign Lands, King, Supreme Lord, Father, Creator, Raging Storm, Wild Bull and Merchant. These titles (especially "Wild Bull") appear to be consistent with the ascription of the horned helmet to Enlil.

It has been argued that, when the winged disc is empty, it represents the Sun but when a figure is inside, it represents Ashur, the state god. What is even more unclear is whether there is any connection at all with the parallel Egyptian symbol of the winged disc but some scholars say the Egyptian one is the source of the others. Later on, the winged disc with the figure inside became a symbol for Zoroastrianism (see appendix two). This is interesting as there is a similarity between the names and nature of both Ashur and Ahura-Mazda (the supreme and good God of Light of the Zoroastrians)[49]. Whether or not this is mere coincidence, it may in any case be possible that Assyrian influence helped to bring about this dramatic reform of polytheistic Persian religion.

Key points

- The Babylonians believed in the existence of demons, notably four-winged Pazuzu
- Their obsession with omens led to animal sacrifices and astrology

- Families of specialist priests controlled each type of divination
- The early astrology was based mainly on planetary omens and lacked numerical accuracy
- As more data was needed, astrology became more complex
- The zodiac was a late development
- Astrology was for the King so magical rituals were devised and used to avert evil omens such as eclipses
- Symbols of the Gods appear on boundary stones and stelae of the Kings

Chapter 7

A Guide to the Mesopotamian Planets[50]

Ninurta: the Babylonian Saturn, holder of the tablets of law, god of sunrise, Lord of Swine, star of law and order.[51]
The symbol of Ninurta or Ninib was the eagle, with either one or two heads (which is the modern symbol for Albania). Variations include a weapon with an eagle's head or an eagle with a lion's head. Sometimes he is portrayed as a man holding a seven-headed weapon. His sacred animal was the pig (which may be the origin of the later taboo on pork). This god and his brother Mars were warrior gods. The planet Saturn was called Sagush or Kayamanu but Ninurta is the god associated with the planet.

The eternal laws had been written by the gods upon the tablets of fate. The power of fate was conferred upon the owner of these tablets. Enlil, the Air god, wore them upon his breast. At dawn one day he removed the tablets in order to wash. They were stolen by Zu, the winged storm dragon, who was in league with Tiamat, the sea dragon of chaos. The gods were too scared to pursue the dragon Zu. Only Ninurta volunteered to be a hero and rescue them. He located Zu's nest in the mountains and saw the tablets hidden within. He brought them back to the great meeting hall of the gods and was rewarded by custody of the tablets. (It sounds as if they were expecting another attempted theft and were happy to let Ninurta deal with it!) This made Ninurta the overseer of fate and destiny or *shimtu* as it was known to the Assyrians. Thus the star Saturn was called the star of law and order. He was the only god who would stand up to chaos.

The Old Testament has a taboo against eating pork, which may be a way of rejecting Ninurta. In the Book of Amos the prophet condemns people for the worship of Sakkut, another name for Ninurta. He was therefore worshiped by some of the Israelites in the 8th century BC; otherwise the criticism would not have been made.

Astrologers called this planet the star of the Sun (Shamash) and the Star of Akkad. It was seen as lucky for the king, who was the prime law-giver. Confusion with the Sun may explain odd reports of seeing the Sun at night – presumably these must refer to Saturn.

Marduk: the Babylonian Jupiter, Saviour of Babylon, father of Nabu (Mercury)[52]

Marduk or Merodach, as described in his Chapter 13 by Baigent, was the city god of Babylon and was associated with the planet Jupiter. The planet Jupiter was called Neberu, the ferry. Marduk's great festival held at the Spring Equinox is the origin of the modern Persian and Kurdish festival of Newroz and possibly also of Passover and Easter.

The New Year in Assyria and Babylonia took place in the Spring. Close to the Spring Equinox, when day and night are of equal length, and the light of warm summer seems to be winning the perpetual struggle against the darkness of cold winter, many of the world's great festivals take place. The first month of the year, *Nisannu*, began with the evening nearest to the spring equinox upon which the crescent moon was first visible. The priests of Babylon would study the sky each evening until the crescent moon was seen. Then they would officially declare the beginning of the month. The first eleven days of *Nisannu* were marked by a great annual festival. The complete details are only known for days two to five. The festival comprised two important rites which were anciently seen as separate festivals – the sacred marriage and the events at the Akitu temple. Similar spring festivals were held at Asshur, Nineveh, Ur, Uruk, Dilbat, Arbela and Harran, so it was very widespread through Babylonia, Assyria and even in the Syrian town of Harran.

On day four, the high priest arose hours before sunrise and with others waited in the temple forecourt for the rising of the constellation known as "the Acre". This appearance was celebrated by chanting a special litany. In the same evening, the creation myth, the *Enuma Elish*, was recited in its entirety by the high priest to the statue of Marduk.

On the fifth day the high priest was allowed to slap the king on his face and pull sharply on his ears. The king was required to kneel before the god and declare that in the past year he had not neglected the temple or the city, he had not sinned and had not offended the native born citizens of the free cities. His face was then struck a second time. Obviously this rite confirms that royalty is in the gift of Marduk and can be taken back at any time.

On the evening of the ninth day is probably when the sacred marriage was celebrated, on top of a ziggurat in the "room of the bed". A priestess took the place of the goddess. Herodotus suggested that this was a symbolic event but if he was wrong, any resulting child would have been born at the winter solstice. As I described in chapter 4, that winter festival has a long history in other parts of the world.

Jupiter was known as either Sagmegar or the Star of Marduk. Jupiter has always been interpreted as a benefic planet. Jupiter/Marduk was seen as king of the gods in many ancient cultures but in astrology the planet does not have a pre-eminent position.

Nergal: the Babylonian Mars, judge of the dead and god of pestilence[53]

In the Assyrian library, scholars knew Mars as Nibeanu or Dugur. The planet was also referred to as Salbatanu, whose meaning is unknown.

Nergal was brother to Ninurta but considered to be evil, lord of both the fires of hell and the heat of fierce summers. His earliest form is the Sumerian deity Lugalmeslam. The translation of this name is "King of the lower world where the Sun lay at night". A very early Sumerian story tells of Nergal and the underworld. The gods gathered in heaven for a great feast. They wanted to invite Ereshkigal, goddess of the underworld. They suggested that she send an emissary to accept her share of food, since they knew she would not leave her domain. When the envoy arrived, all the other gods rose to greet him but Nergal snubbed him by remaining firmly seated. This insult to the goddess made her angry. She asked for Nergal's life. Nergal appealed but had to make the journey down to the underworld to face execution. He took 14 companions, one for each of the doors of her palace. (This is a mirror image of the early Kabbalah ascent stories.) He put one companion on guard at each door. On entry to the place he found the envoy and killed him. He then found Ereshkigal, dragged her to the floor and was about to slice off her head. She pleaded with him and offered marriage. He dried her tears and accepted her offer. From then on they jointly ruled over the underworld, Arallu.

Like Ninurta, Nergal was seen as a war god, a god of battle. So we have a prediction, "when a planet and Mars stand facing one another, there will be an invasion of the enemy." He ruled cattle, and in modern astrology Mars still rules abattoirs and butchers. In modern astrology, however, the planet Pluto is connected with the underworld.

Shamash: the Babylonian Sun, judge of heaven and earth[54]

His symbol is the equal-armed cross, possibly representing the four quarters of the year, often shown within a circle. This symbol was worn around the neck of the king. (However, according to one report from the Assyrian scholars to the King, the cross is the emblem of the god Nabu. This may refer to Nabu in his role as crown prince.)

His sacred wood was tamarisk, used to make his statues. Shamash was the brother of Ishtar and son of Sin.

This must have been an important god in astrology since twelve tablets in the *Enuma Anu Enlil* are devoted to the Sun.

The Sun god was treated as Supreme Judge in cultic rituals such as the *Namburbi* ritual. A solar eclipse was evil for the king and so a ritual was invented to divert the harm. A substitute king reigned, usually for 100 days, and then went to his fate. This usually happened every 3 or 4 years. In 671 BC it happened twice and each substitute was killed[55]. The rituals involved prayers, ceremonies, chants, incense – like a full-blown exorcism.

How did a person come to be appointed as substitute king? In Assyria, it was the custom to give a prominent temple office to a citizen. This would bring him into contact with the cult and the gods. Such a man might serve as substitute for the king when an eclipse afflicting the land of Akkad took place. There was a ritualized coronation ceremony, the substitute then took upon himself all the ill omens and thereafter ruled in silence to the end of his time.

One such substitute, called Damqi, who had ruled Assyria, Babylonia and all the countries, went to his destiny and was apparently killed[56]. Records show that there was a burial chamber prepared. He and his queen were decorated, treated, displayed, buried and wailed over.

The throne, table weapon and scepter would be burned at this time and the ashes buried "at their head", with the probable meaning of by the king and queen. Then six paired wooden statues were constructed. A formula was written on the left hip of each statue, simply saying, depart evil and enter good. Each of them was buried and life returned to normal.

Ishtar: the Babylonian Venus, Queen of Heaven[57]

The planet Venus was known as Dilbat, whose meaning is unknown. Ancient people knew that Venus was found close to the Sun but had regular periods of invisibility. These periods of absence lasted 50 days. A view to the east from a high point overlooking water would provide the best conditions for spotting her return, where the high angle slightly prolongs the period Venus can be seen safely before the sunrise, so astronomers would have favoured the siting of observatories in such locations. This would entail a whole community and a temple being established. The rising of Venus marked the start of a new 260 day orbital cycle. This is the kind of observational astronomy we find in the *Venus Tablet* of Babylonian King Amisaduqa. One site which has a Temple of Venus on a cliff is the Greek colony of Tyndaris in Sicily.[58] The Greeks were certainly not the first to use this effect because the Sumerian city of Eridu was dedicated to Venus (as Inanna/Ishtar) and the view across its harbour to the east would also have allowed the return of Venus to be observed.

Ishtar's official cult centre was in the city of Uruk but she was worshiped widely throughout the Middle East. The origins of this deity are extremely complicated. The Semitic newcomers brought a male deity Attar which gradually assumed the characteristics of Sumerian Inanna and was known as Ishtar. She was the third deity in the triad with Sin and Shamash. She was the sister of both Shamash and Ereshkigal.

While Inanna had many aspects, the essence of Ishtar was to be Goddess of Love. Ishtar's cult spread to Cyprus where she was called Aphrodite and when she reached Rome she took the name Venus. A number of important figures in the Greco-Roman world claimed descent from Venus.

She was worshipped by King Solomon who wrote:

"Who is this arising like the dawn
fair as the moon
resplendent as the Sun
terrible as an army with banners?"

Venus (the planet known as Dilbat) was known as the goat-star and ruled fertility. The entry of Venus into the constellation Libra (around the Autumn equinox) was seen as a portent of war. Venus ruled over women and the success of the harvest.

Nabu: the Babylonian Mercury/Hermes, scribe of the gods, swift herald[59]

Nabu or Nebo was the equivalent of the Egyptian god Thoth (Tehuti). His symbol was most commonly the writing desk but also the mason's chisel or a measuring rod. The planet Mercury was known as Sihtu, which means jumping.

The Spring Festival

Every Spring when the Sun entered Aries, there was a festival in Babylon in honour of Marduk[60]. On the 7th day of the festival, Nabu rescued Marduk from imprisonment. On the 11th day, when the gods assembled to decide the fate of the world for the next year, it was Nabu who recorded them.

The sky was the book of the gods, *shitir shame*, where fate could be read. Hence the later astrological practice of assessing the chart for the Aries Ingress to forecast the year ahead. (The first point of Aries is believed to be politically significant and the EU's chart has the Sun in that position.)

The Temple at Borsippa

The explorer Henry Rawlinson copied cuneiform inscriptions off a dangerous rock face at Behistun and was the first modern to translate and read Assyrian[61]. In 1854 he went to Borsippa south of Babylon where he uncovered the remains of the temple of Nabu. He noticed that the stages of the temple were coloured differently and that it was a ziggurat structure. The base level was coloured black and six others lay above it. Cylinders buried in the foundations for good luck recorded that the Temple was dedicated to "the planets of the 7 spheres" and it was called "The stages of the seven spheres".[62]

The Sabaean Planetary Order

Sir Henry Rawlinson reconstructed the full scheme in accordance with the Sabaean planetary scheme. The Sabaeans were a religious group during the 6th to 10th centuries AD who were based in Harran, a major city on the route from Assyria and Babylonia to the Mediterranean. They had retained much ancient star lore, as noted by Moses Maimonides in "Guide for the Perplexed". The sequence used by the Sabaeans matches that used by modern Qabalists when putting the planets on the Tree of Life, so this Sabaean system is different from that attributed to the ancient Assyrians by Professor Parpola. But it would have to be so, because the Sephiroth of the Tree did not originate as planets but as numbers. Similar Temples existed in Harran, dedicated for example to the moon (Sin). The sequence in the Sabaean planetary order is that of *speed of planetary motion*, starting at the base with the slowest, Saturn, and ending at the summit with the moon, as the fastest and Father of the Gods. The table is also useful for showing how the names of the planetary omens started in Mesopotamia, were translated into Greek and later taken up by the Romans. The continuity of meaning remained.

Chart of Nabu Temple Correspondences

Planet	Brick colour	Sephirah	Babylon God	Greek God
Saturn	Black	3	Ninurta	Kronos
Jupiter	Red-brown	4	Marduk	Zeus
Mars	Bright red	5	Nergal	Ares
Sun/Sol	Gold?	6	Shamash	Apollon
Venus	Yellow	7	Ishtar	Aphrodite
Mercury	Blue	8	Nabu	Hermes
Moon/Luna	Silver?	9	Sin	Selene/Diana

Sin: Babylonian Moon God, Chief of the Gods, Father of Time[63]

The moon god was Nanna to the Sumerians and Sin to the Akkadians. Day emerged from night, and light emerged from the darkness. So Sin was seen as father of the Sun and Venus. As it says in Genesis: "And darkness was upon the face of the deep. And the Spirit of God moved upon the face of the waters. And God said, "Let there be light"."

Sin's symbol of the lunar crescent was carved upon most of the stelae of the Kings. Quite often there is an arc joining the tips, to complete the circle.

Sin ruled over time and the calendar. The first 22 tablets of the *Enuma Anu Enlil* series referred to lunar omens. Sin had particular wisdom causing him to be consulted by the other gods, rather like Odin in the Nordic tradition.

The lunar month was broken up into groups of seven days. So the seventh, fourteenth, nineteenth (oddly), twenty-first and twenty-eighth days were especially significant and dangerous. This is the origin of the taboo of the Sabbath. The day of the Full moon was given over to rejoicing and prayer. That day was named *Shabattu* and it is the source of the Hebrew word *Shabbat* and the English term Sabbath.

The supreme cult centres of Sin were at Ur in Babylonia and Harran in Syria. Terah, the father of Abraham, according to the Book of Genesis, left his home city of Ur, planning to settle in Canaan, but on reaching the trading city of Harran, he settled there, and it was only later that Abraham completed the trek. There was a tendency to make Sin the supreme god and even monotheistic, so the Sin cult could well have been a major influence on the development of the Hebrew religion. (There are, of course, other theories, such as those based on the Egyptian Aten cult of Akhenaten.)

In the British Museum, there is a stela of Nabonidus, the last King of Babylon before the Persian conquest. He was son of the priestess of Sin at Harran. He tried unsuccessfully to convert Harran's moon worship into the national cult of Babylonia.

It is significant that Sin is often addressed as Father and Mount Sinai is arguably an old cult centre of Sin, where Moses was said to have received the tablets of the law and the Golden Calf was worshiped.

What often strikes students who go on my tours of the British Museum is the fact that the moon is male, in India and the Near East, whereas in European (Roman and Greek) astrology, the moon is *always* seen as female (although I am aware of northern moon gods). This is because the Europeans tended in the main to see the moon as female, for example, as Diana, Selene, Arianrhod (which means silver wheel), and Luna. From a European perspective, it seems obvious that the moon would be feminine, because of the monthly cycle of fertility. Robert Graves would have had deep trouble trying to compose his mythological arguments in "The White Goddess"[64] if he had extended its scope to deal with this issue!

Why this difference exists between Europe and the Near East is a fascinating question and I hope that it will be investigated adequately and findings will be published. In my experience, there is a real hunger to understand this distinction. Perhaps the emphasis on the moon in this region is connected with the specific needs of navigation in large expanses of utterly featureless desert, where the moon is the only reliable basis for measurement beyond the East/West journey of the Sun overhead, and where travel is in fact easier at night due to the absence of the Sun's heat. My hypothesis is that the Bedouin tribes always have one leader, a sheikh, who is male, and so may have drawn an analogy between the tribe and the planets, giving the night sky a male leader. Similarly, the Germanic moon god may have been worshipped by a tribe which habitually had a male leader.

Astrology, as it developed and moved into Europe via Egypt, changed its emphasis from the moon to the Sun and my theory would be that the Egyptians, who had a predominant solar deity (Amun or Ra), would have done away with the lunar emphasis of the Mesopotamians, leaving the Greeks and Romans to follow suit for similar reasons.

Key points

- Sin the Moon God was worshipped throughout the Near East as Chief of the Planetary Gods but each city had its own special deity
- Moon Gods in the Near East were commonly male, not female
- All the planets had cults and omens attached to them, often consistent with modern astrological interpretations
- Temples were devoted to Planetary Gods
- The Temple of Nabu (Mercury) at Borsippa had coloured steps related to each planet
- The modern Qabalistic order of planets is derived from speed of planetary motion; it is different from the Assyrian sephirothic correspondences

Chapter 8

The Arguments About Ancient Telescopes

We are taught that the ancient astronomers were using the naked eye and did not have the advantage of telescopes, which magnify the stars. One might therefore assume that they had no magnification at all. However, the truth is less straightforward and quite surprising.

Robert Temple, who is a recognized scholar in many fields, a sinologist and an expert on Gilgamesh, has published a very delightful book[65], called *The Crystal Sun*, arguing for the existence of telescopes in the ancient world, which is an intellectual gymnasium if ever there was one.

Arthur C. Clarke, writing an introduction, comments that, "although Galileo is rightly credited with *introducing the telescope to the world* [my italics] in 1609, he certainly did not invent it. As Robert Temple points out in this impressively researched book, excellent rock crystal lenses had been known for several thousand years, and it seems incredible that Archimedes – or some Chinese or Egyptian inventor even earlier – did not make the obvious and simple experiment of looking through two of them at the same time".

Before I summarize his case and give my considered and hopefully not unkind opinion on his very learned conclusions, I would like to summarize the technological history which is relevant.

Telescopes, or so we are taught in school, were first used by Galileo in the 17th century, as a result of which new bodies were discovered in outer space and he was subjected to discipline by the Church for threatening the then current but wrong notion that the earth was at the centre of the solar system.

In order to build telescopes, most of us will assume (and it is only an assumption) that two glass lenses are required. It is therefore necessary to go briefly over the early history of glass-making. Glass was made for thousands of years before glass *blowing* was learnt. I have seen this wonderful skill carried out in Venice and vividly remember the heat generated.

According to Graham Philip, Lecturer in Archaeology at the University of Durham, the early evidence for glass-making goes back to the third millennium BC[66]. The evidence from the Near East includes occasional beads, a piece of blue-white raw glass, a glass rod and a lump of raw blue glass from Eridu (probably the first town in Sumer).

A major change occurred in around 1600 BC, when new techniques and colours appear. Glass vessels must have existed because fragments survive. Hot glass was moulded around a core of straw-tempered mud or a clay-dung mixture. The object was rolled while the glass was soft. The vessels were mostly blue with decoration in yellow and white. When the glass cooled, the core was scraped out. Glass then was obviously a luxury, high-status material. Although much glassware was found at Nuzi, a Hurrian site, opinion is divided as to whether the supposed association of glass with the Hurrians is valid. Besides vessels, glass was employed for the manufacture of amulets, pendants, figurines and beads imitating precious stones.

Clear glass, produced in imitation of rock-crystal, appeared in the ancient Near East by 700 BC. Please note this fact because rock-crystal is very important in Robert Temple's theory, and clear glass makes theoretically possible the production of a glass lens and therefore clearer magnification than was possible with rock-crystal. Other innovations continued to appear but this is a key fact, so I will stop here.

Robert Temple does not state this but I have noticed (see my timeline) that in the following century a great leap forward occurred in astronomy in that region – including the compilation of *Mul Apin* and the start of astronomical diaries. Perhaps these facts are suggestive of some actual technical advance, simple magnification or even full-scale telescope use? However, there is a weakness in this line of argument, because the *Mul Apin* has been proved by scholars to be drawn from much earlier sources, well before 700 BC. Nevertheless, the fact that it was compiled at all and that astronomical diaries started to be kept is still suggestive of a change in understanding and possibly also of technology that would cause such a change in understanding.

One alternative explanation of that indisputable change of understanding would be a realization that earlier records were inadequate and were not giving the King the reliable forecasts which would both satisfy him and maintain the star priests in their privileged posts. This is the hypothesis expounded by Michael Baigent[67], based on his own readings of scholarship. If the priests of those days already believed that astrology could potentially work better than it actually did, they would be in a similar intellectual position to those modern astrologers who either try to use statistical analysis of astrological techniques to test what works or else devise new methods (either invented or drawn from different cultures) in the hope of improving its effectiveness. One could draw up quite a long list of alternative methods of astrology promoted in the modern world, which differ very greatly from the classical tradition. There has been a reaction: one of the most interesting manifestations of the modern dissatisfaction with mainstream astrology is a concerted effort by numbers of the most intellectually able astrologers to translate and then teach from traditional texts, which are classical or medieval in provenance, thus putting them for the first time within reach of the student. This is truly watering the roots of the tree.

The first lens which Robert Temple analyses in detail is the Layard lens[68] (object no. 12091 in the British Museum Department of Western Asiatic Antiquities). It was excavated by Austen Henry Layard in 1849 in the North-West Palace of the ancient Assyrian capital of Kalhu (called Nimrud). He determined that it was from the reign of Sargon II in the latter part of the 7th century BC. One of the objects found here, near the royal throne itself, was a rock-crystal lens, with opposite convex and plane faces. Layard wrote, "Its properties could scarcely have been unknown to the Assyrians, and we have consequently the earliest specimen of a magnifying and burning glass." There were chippings on the edge to suggest that it had been pried out of a valuable metal band, so it was mounted but not backed.

Temple concludes that it was not effective for a burning glass. It can magnify to 1.25X and would enable a mildly long-sighted person to read without spectacles. It is quite possible that the Layard lens was used as a monocle by Sargon II or his chief scribe. Troy, Ephesus and Knossos had large numbers of ground crystal lenses, so a visiting craftsman from such a location could have made the lens for the Assyrian palace.

The book continues with lists of crystal lenses on display in museums abroad, categorised as decorative jewellery, which may really be optical glasses. There are literally hundreds of these. He also examines (in chapters 2-5) helpful ancient literary sources which, so he hopes, may have been mistranslated, because of a prejudice against the possible existence of ancient telescopes.

One intriguing discovery (at *Temple* pp. 147-148) is about Roger Bacon, who lived in the 13th century when the key lost book we need here, the *Optics* of Ptolemy, still existed. Bacon seems to have constructed a telescope at Oxford, which led to his being accused of witchcraft. The French historian of astronomy, Jean Sylvain Bailly, says that Father Jean Mabillon had seen a 13th century manuscript by a monk called Conrad, stating that Conrad had come across an ancient manuscript which contained an illustration of *Claudius Ptolemy (2nd century AD) looking at the stars through a long tube*. Bailly thinks that the star catalogues compiled by Hipparchus and Ptolemy were done with individual star observations made through long tubes. Bailly imagined that these tubes were made of paper but of course (says Temple, who is an expert on China) paper was a Chinese invention and did not exist in Europe prior to the 11th century.

I observe that (1) this is at several degrees of hearsay (2) an image on a manuscript is not strong proof as it may be imaginative like a drawing of a unicorn and (3) if these tubes were telescopes, as Temple hopes, they were not well used, because it is agreed by scholars that ancient Egyptian astronomy always lagged behind that of Babylon and Greece. It is therefore most unlikely that they used two lenses, in my opinion, if the image is even anything more than imagination.

Further points struck me, which are, firstly, that Ptolemy worked in Egypt and was not a European by birth (although an ethnic Greek). Secondly, this raises the possibility of papyrus tubes, which I cannot see referenced in his index. The word paper comes directly from papyrus. The Greek word for book is *biblos*, named after the ancient town of Byblos on the coast of Phoenicia. People in these regions were writing on paper *before* Ptolemy, hence the Dead Sea Scrolls and the Nag Hammadi "Gnostic Gospels". Papyrus is made by mashing up reeds (found in rivers like the Nile, adjacent to Ptolemy's home) into a pulp and then drying the paste in the hot sun until it sets. It would be very easy to make a tube of papyrus if required.

Furthermore, I was very much aware of the ancient Egyptian astronomical tradition, having spent days in the British Museum and elsewhere researching it for an article and book reviews that I wrote some years ago. The ceilings of several ancient Egyptian monuments have astronomical ceilings, star maps overhead modeled on the night sky. We know that certain stars were of great importance in the ancient Egyptian religion, that these Egyptians had measuring astronomical instruments and that their astronomical headquarters was at Heliopolis or On, located underneath a suburb of modern Cairo and not far from the Giza plateau, which is always at the centre of astronomical speculations (such as, most famously, the Orion Mystery).

The tomb ceiling of a very important 19th Dynasty Pharaoh, Seti I, who lived in the century immediately before the probable time of Moses, was found in the Valley of the Kings. It was extensively photographed before it was sealed off for safety reasons. This ceiling is almost our earliest Egyptian star map and therefore very important in the history of astronomy. I have my own ideas about what it represents, which I have published elsewhere. It displays a number of constellations with red spots to mark individual stars. At the heart of it lie the undying stars, the circumpolar constellations which never set. This has often made me wonder if the Egyptians knew enough to determine that the equinoctial point (which they clearly knew about as we can judge from alignments of monumental structures) was slowly precessing through the ages. An argument against that speculation would be that they did not use the Babylonian zodiac until very late, when the invasions from Asia of the 1st millennium BC ended their independence. This influence is apparent in the Denderah zodiac, which uses the zodiac mixed in with the Seti I stars, dating from only about 2,000 years ago and therefore no help at all. A word of caution here: we cannot assume that Seti I star patterns which resemble a lion or a bull or other birds and beasts are anything to do with the Babylonian constellations of the same name. These two traditions very obviously have different roots. And the Egyptian star maps *are not drawn to scale*. Like all Egyptian art, subject to usually rigid conventions, they were more abstract and more perfect and simpler than the reality portrayed. I may be wrong about precession, as Jane B Sellers, who has studied the mythological implications of Egyptian astronomy in great depth, believes that the Egyptians did not know about it, as she states in her fascinating book[69], "The Death of Gods in Ancient Egypt".

Hipparchus and Ptolemy may very well have used some instruments to survey the stars but there were tools *other than the telescope* in use by Egyptian astronomers. Obviously the telescope would have been best, if it was available. The tradition refers to other tools. I therefore conclude that telescopes were not used.

Let us return to the Layard lens, in order to consider further the question of ancient telescopes. In 1930, the distinguished optician W.B.Barker, President of what is today called the College of Optometrists in London, dedicated an entire article to the "Nineveh lens". I have paraphrased slightly (for ease of reading) a section of it (p.17, *Temple*) where he referred to: "R. Campbell Thompson's published reports of the "Astronomers of Nineveh and Babylon" which were found recorded on a large number of tablets from the mid 7th century BC. On these tablets are found records of observations of the planet Dilbat, which cannot (*sic*) be seen with the naked eye, but is visible with the aid of a fairly strong glass. This fact led to the further suggestion that lenses such as this were used by the ancient astronomers who must have called to their aid some optical apparatus for magnifying..."

Temple rightly states that the planet called Dilbat[70] is now thought to be Venus, which certainly does not require a telescope to be seen. Mr Barker's reported opinion was wrong, in my view, on this one matter. Venus is often the brightest planet visible in the night sky and her symbol was often inscribed on Mesopotamian carvings (on display in the British Museum and elsewhere), as she was linked to a major Goddess. With respect to Mr Barker, I do not find observations of Venus to be a credible basis for arguing telescopes into existence in Babylon. I will acknowledge that Babylonian astronomers, who held hereditary posts and worked for very demanding Kings, were under great pressure to make their observations as reliable and thorough as they possibly could, so they would have had a strong motive to use the best available technology and even to invent more[71]. It is common knowledge that an electric battery, for example, was invented and constructed in Babylonia.

Intriguingly, Temple goes on: *"But the question of "invisible" outer planets, of the Galilean moons of Jupiter and of the rings of Saturn being familiar to ancient astronomers is one which has never been entirely resolved, together with the possibility of rudimentary telescopes in antiquity. Amongst both the ancient Greeks and the ancient Chinese there were traditions implying an astronomical knowledge of these two planetary phenomena in our solar system which cannot be discerned by the naked eye."*

I am completely unaware of any such tradition, despite considerable study of the world of ancient Greece and its astronomy. I would expect any such reference to have been made by Ptolemy in the magisterial (but fallible) *Almagest* but that text is not cited in support of the argument. Robert Temple does not set out the evidence for these assertions in that book, or at least I failed to find that he had done so. His footnote takes the reader instead to his earlier work, *The Sirius Mystery*, where the curious reader can follow.

My reaction at this point is to note that the surviving astrological and astronomical tradition, as codified in particular by Ptolemy, which is consistent in its interpretations of specific planets as specific omens from ancient Mesopotamia to the Middle Ages and beyond, *does not speak of the outer planets until they were discovered in modern times*. Furthermore, astrologers attach great significance to the modern name and the year of discovery of the outer planets: thus Uranus, for example, is interpreted in the light of the relevant Greek myth and the revolutions which happened in the late 18th century.

All the surviving records of early astronomical observations *which have so far been translated* are, to the best of my knowledge, of the Sun and moon, known planets out to Saturn and known fixed stars. If there was even one definite and indisputable ancient observation on record of Uranus (the next planet) or an invisible moon of Jupiter or the rings of Saturn, would it not be found in all the histories of astronomy/astrology and be the subject of avid research by departments of archaeo-astronomy? It just needs one example to prove his argument, no more. Perhaps there is some still untranslated cuneiform text in the British Museum which will put this issue to rest but the omission from the known texts (such as *Mul Apin*) is rather telling. I will wish him the best of luck in his quest and, in a positive scientific way, I would very much like to see experiments carried out with *contemporary* binoculars and telescopes made with rock-crystal lenses, to put these theories to the test. There must be a School, College or University somewhere which would like the honour. And then we might also settle the interesting question of what Roger Bacon did at Oxford.

The heliocentric solar system drawn by Copernicus was not an entirely new understanding. Sadly, the influence of Ptolemy, who mistakenly favoured the geocentric system, had left no room for dissident thinkers. Prior to Ptolemy, a Greek astronomer called Aristarchus had also proposed the theory that the earth went around the Sun[72]. If telescopes had been widely available at that time, perhaps the history of astronomy would have taken a very different course. This issue, among others, such as the lack of proven knowledge of trans-Saturnian planets, inclines me to doubt quite strongly that Ptolemy had an effective telescope in his possession.

Key points

- Telescopes might have been made from rock crystal before glass lenses were available but if so proof of their effectiveness is elusive
- In Naqada II period Egypt, 5,300 years ago, rock carvings appeared, the earliest example of art which is impossible without magnification
- Rock crystal was used to make an effective eyeglass for an

important person in Assyria with defective vision

- Museums contain hundreds of ancient crystal lenses which are often wrongly identified as jewellery
- Clear glass was not produced until the 7th century BC but opaque glass was made for millennia beforehand
- Ptolemy may have used a telescope (2nd century AD) according to Robert Temple (disputed)
- In the 13th century Roger Bacon may have made a telescope at Oxford

Chapter 9

Origins Of The Constellations

Each civilized culture tends to arrange the stars into groups and give the group a name. Most of our modern constellations were named for us by the Greeks, who supported the name with a lively myth or two involving the character represented. We can find evidence pointing to Sumer and Babylonia as the origins of the Greek constellation myths. This is an interesting story in itself.

When I was a schoolboy I very much enjoyed reading the *Metamorphoses* of Ovid, one of Rome's most entertaining, if tragic, poets. This was a collection of Greek tales of transformation strongly connected with the star myths of the constellations[73]. It often explained why character A was facing character B in the heavens and it was both a bardic tool and a practical help for navigation by the stars at night. The Greek culture from whose sources he drew was of course a culture of people living on numerous islands and craggy coastlines, requiring excellent navigation skills. This accident of geography means that even in the present day Greece has a pre-eminent position in the world of shipping – one thinks, for example, of the late Aristotle Onassis. The most famous Greek legends, like the Odyssey and the Voyage of the Argo, are stories of sailors dealing with unimaginable challenges in distant lands.

One of the main themes of Greek myth was the distinction between the mortals (humans) and the immortals (gods). Occasionally a very special person might be placed in the heavens as a permanent, immortal, star spirit. This theme of ascension into the heavens has interesting parallels in Egyptian, Kabbalistic and Mesopotamian beliefs. My impression is that the ancient Greeks borrowed freely from other cultures and their consolidation of this earlier knowledge is therefore perhaps not entirely accurately represented as the origin of European civilization. In my investigations into Greek science I have found many examples of Greek thinkers receiving the credit for concepts which were not new to them. One example is the 19-year eclipse cycle known as the Metonic cycle, named after Meton of Athens. Thousands of years before he lived, this cycle was clearly known to the builders of Stonehenge[74]. What I cannot say is whether there was direct transmission or that this was an independent discovery.

The constellation system that we use today is based on the list of 48 constellations published around 150 AD in Ptolemy's book the *Almagest* (from its name in Arabic translation). Another 40 have been added since then, making a current total of 88 constellations. There are in fact nearly two dozen other "temporary" constellations that fell by the wayside.

Claudius Ptolemy (whose first name probably commemorates the famous 1st century Roman Emperor and conqueror of Britain) wrote the main textbook on astronomy for succeeding generations. From its Arabic name we can be sure that its central importance worldwide lasted into the Middle Ages. Map makers in Europe and Arabia used Ptolemy for over 1,500 years. Astronomy was one of the essential subjects in the educational curriculum of Europe in the Middle Ages. In other words, this was a publisher's dream – a best seller that never lost its position in the market. However, Ptolemy was not a great originator. He was a compiler. He had access to the great library of Alexandria, the best in the world, and not only did he use Greek texts but – crucially - he was referring to cuneiform tablets, which he had the ability to read, despite the very different language. He had direct access to the already fading traditions of the Babylonian *tupsharru* star priests[75]. Berossus was one such, who had brought his library with him to the Greek island of Cos. Ptolemy specifically wrote in volumes III and IV of the *Almagest* that he had access to eclipse records dating from the era of Nabonassar, King of Babylon from 747 to 734 BC. He complained about the lack of reliable planetary data. He was disappointed that the observations recorded the appearances and disappearances of planets and stars, all of which were difficult to observe. (In fact the Babylonians themselves were unhappy and from the 7th century BC to at least the 1st century BC we have detailed diaries in which a much fuller picture of heavenly and earthly events is recorded by the astronomers, which, as Michael Baigent[76] has commented, looks like an attempt to create a database.) So the *Almagest* is an encyclopaedia of Greek and Babylonian astronomy, as it was understood in the 2nd century AD at the world centre of education. This was a "must have" book for every astronomer[77].

I should explain who Claudius Ptolemy was *not* as his name often causes confusion. Alexander the Great conquered the Near East in the late 4th century BC. His Macedonian troops spoke a dialect of Greek. The culture which they imposed is usually called *Hellenistic* for this reason. After Alexander's death, the Empire was divided between heirs, so that his General, Ptolemy, ruled Egypt like the Pharaohs, with a dynasty, many of whom took his name in their turn. This was the cosmopolitan world into which Ptolemy the astronomer, Jesus and the Disciples, Queen Cleopatra and many other striking Roman era personalities were born.

The area that the Hellenistic dynasties controlled was huge: in addition to the usual Near Eastern Empire of Turkey, the Levant, Egypt and Iraq, it extended eastwards at its maximum extent through Persia and Afghanistan as far as India and north into what are now some of the southern states of Russia. Alexander was always on the move, always seeking new countries. The dynasty of the Ptolemies ruled Egypt for centuries and ended with Cleopatra, who played power games with the rulers of Rome as its Republic gave way to the Empire. Ptolemy the astronomer lived under the Roman rule which followed after Cleopatra but as far as we know he was not of the royal lineage. Many Greeks continued to live in the important cities of Egypt, as the ruling class, and Ptolemy was obviously a popular choice for a boy's name. The fact that he had both a Latin and a Greek name shows how much the ruling class was insulated from the Egyptian majority and also how important it was to keep "well in" with the Roman rulers. We should not assume that the European-descended ruling class was normally privy to any secrets of "ancient Egyptian mysteries", and of course anything written down in the Library of Alexandria was not a mystery at that time.

The constellations listed in the *Almagest* are much older than Ptolemy's era. But the early Greek writers, Homer and Hesiod (7th century BC) mentioned only a few star groups, such as the Great Bear, Orion and the Pleiades star cluster. The rising of the Pleiades near the Spring Equinox was a very important seasonal marker in ancient Europe and the Near East. Homer and Hesiod did not write about the Babylonian zodiac at all and it is therefore likely that they were unaware of it.

A much better list is found in the *Mul Apin* series, a star list written in cuneiform on clay tablets around 700 BC. This lists the star groups on what we would call, after the Greek term, the zodiac band, across which travels the Sun, moon and planets. These are mostly identical with the modern star groups. Other historical research has established that the constellations known to the Babylonians originated much earlier, with the Sumerians, before 2000 BC. The *Mul Apin* is a two-tablet compilation whose astronomy dates from 1000 BC or earlier, according to work carried out by Professors Reiner and Pingree at the Chicago planetarium[78]. Forty different examples of the text are known, of various dates. Only two of them contain a definite date, the earliest of these being from 687 BC. Therefore we have a difficulty that this is the earliest date from which we can be sure that the information was arranged into this compilation.

It is grouped into 18 sections. These include a list of fixed stars divided into those of the paths of Ea, Anu and Enlil, the dates when the 36 fixed stars and constellations rise in the morning, the planetary periods, the seasons, equinoxes and solstices, tables of the period of the moon's visibility, rules for intercalation, gnomon tables detailing shadow lengths and weights of water for their water-clocks. There are also some omens, drawn from comets and fixed stars. Furthermore, we have a hint of a zodiac: it lists all the stars in the "path of the moon". This was a list of 18 constellations, which later fell to 12 and then was changed into 12 equal divisions, or zodiac signs. (Zodiac means the circle of living creatures, which are the predominant type of constellation on this band, from *zoe* meaning life in Greek.)

The first clear evidence we have of an extensive set of Greek constellations comes from the astronomer *Eudoxus* (c.390-340 BC). Eudoxus[79] was taught by the Egyptian priests. At this time Egypt was controlled by the Persians. The Persians were Zoroastrians by religion (see appendix two) and influenced at this time by the legacy of the Babylonians and Assyrians. This was the kind of astronomy and religious attitude which they brought into Egypt. The story of Eudoxus (who was taught at On by Ichonuphys) also tells us that the Egyptian priests of the 4th century BC had maintained an astronomical tradition. It seems likely that the priests in question would have been based at the placed named by the Greeks as On (Heliopolis) or in Biblical Hebrew as On or Awen, in what is now southern Cairo. The focus of these priests would have been on the calendar rather than on divination. Fixing the calendar by reference to the stars was a major goal of these priests.[80] On was largely uninhabited by the 1st century BC, according to Strabo, although its priests still lingered; Alexandria had supplanted it in importance.

Tragically, the two works of Eudoxus which we would want

to read are both lost. Luckily the *Phaenomena* survives in a poem of the same name by Aratus of c.315-c.245 BC. This means that Aratus is our main guide to the Greek constellations[81].

Aratus was a student at Athens. He went to the Court of King Antigonus of Macedon in northern Greece. He wrote his poem around 275 BC and identified 47 constellations. Now we have a clue like "Sherlock Holmes and the dog that didn't bark". From the constellations which he does *not* describe, we can deduce that the constellation makers must have lived at a latitude of about 36 degrees north, which is south of Greece but north of Egypt, thus conveniently ruling out from our enquiries both Greece and Egypt!

A further clue is the fact that this "constellation-free" zone was centered on the south celestial pole but *not at the time Aratus lived*. The position of the pole was more than 1,500 years before him, at around 2000 BC. The position of the celestial pole changes of course with time because of the Earth's axial wobble, known as precession. Thus the evidence points to invention of the constellations described by Aratus around 2000 BC by people who lived close to latitude 36 degrees north. This rules out continental Europeans and Africans completely because it is on the latitude of the Mediterranean (unless you include island civilisations such as Minoans from Crete or the Maltese or Cypriots). It turns the spotlight on Asia. The best evidence for a well-developed astronomy at that latitude in that period is however in the sites of the Babylonians and Sumerians. The widest possible range of locations will always come back to a culture living at their latitude. I am reluctant to dispute Sumer because, if a Mediterranean island had invented these constellations, it seems odd that Homer and Hesiod were unaware of them, whereas there were many more stars recorded in the astronomy-obsessed culture of Iraq.

Alan Butler has argued that the Phaistos Disc from Crete is a calendar[82] based on 366 days and that the Cretans invented the

zodiac and used telescopes. However, these views are controversial and I was not persuaded to change my opinion by the
arguments as presented. Readers will need to evaluate his
evidence and make up their own minds. I hope that the information I present here will help. Apart from this interpretation of
the Phaistos disc and the arguments in Alan Butler's book, there
is no other evidence, to my knowledge, that the Minoans were
interested in astronomy. This may not be conclusive – after all,
their civilization was wiped out by a catastrophe.

Professor Archie Roy of Glasgow University has argued that
the Babylonian constellations must have reached Egypt via some
other civilization[83]. I have suggested this was the result of the
Persian conquest of the Near East but Professor Roy proposes the
Minoans of Crete. He notices, I am sure correctly, that the work
of Aratus includes much weather lore of use to navigators. I am
convinced that the Greek star tales were of practical use to them
as sailors. It was difficult to be an ancient Greek and *not* be
involved with the sea. It is omnipresent in the Greek world.

Professor Roy concludes that the seafarers who used the
constellations were the Minoans. They lived on Crete and
Santorini (Thera). Crete lies between 35 and 36 degrees north,
which is the right latitude. The Minoan empire was expanding
between 3000 and 2000 BC, which was the right date. The
Minoans were in contact with the Babylonians through Syria
from an early stage. In 1450 BC the volcanic eruption on Thera
ended the Minoan civilisation. The Minoan refugees went
somewhere else, possibly bringing the Atlantis legend with them
as well as their star lore to Egypt: this is the destination postulated by Professor Roy. It is certainly true that Minoan art occurs
in Egypt, proving the presence of at least one Minoan colony
there.

I visited Crete in 1992. I have often pondered the facial
features shown in Minoan art, which look quite Levantine, with
black curling hair and prominent noses. I was struck by the

unique flavour of Cretan mythology which is distinctive from that elsewhere in the Greek world. God names, you suspect, refer to different entities from those on the mainland. Zeus is supposed to have been reared by the goat Amaltheia in the Mount Dikte cave on the central Lassithi Plateau. There is an emphasis on "birthing caves" which may connect back to the Megalithic birthing chambers of North-Western Europe. There are no wall paintings or star lists to show any interest here in astronomy but the caves are suggestive. Did a particular star need to shine into the cave?

Key points

- The Greeks gave us the constellation myths in the form we know them today
- The important Greek astronomer Ptolemy (who worked in Egypt) had access to Mesopotamian astronomy records, which he could read and use
- Eudoxus and Aratus first wrote up in Greek the legends of the constellations
- The origins of constellation myths lie either in Sumer or alternatively in some Mediterranean island culture, such as Minoan Crete
- They must originate on that latitude, which eliminates both mainland Europe and Egypt
- While the physical evidence for an early interest in astronomy is strongest in Mesopotamia, the sailors of Greece and Minoan Crete made practical use of the stars for navigation at night.

Chapter 10

The Beginning Of The End

What happened to the Assyrians later on? They did not vanish but are still with us, against great odds. They had a difficult task controlling the upper plains of Mesopotamia because they were surrounded by inhabited mountains to the north and east and other mighty cultures to the south and west. Invaders repeatedly threatened them. Despite these challenges, they had an opportunity to rule a great empire, which peaked in the period 750-612 BC, and they left the modern world some outstanding inventions, including the arch (much copied by the Romans), an improved bow weapon and improved chariot (from the simple Sumerian battle wagon), a postal system and the provincial organisation of their empire (later copied by, among others, the Persians, Greeks and Romans). This used the management technique of delegation; a loyal governor in the province was much more efficient than direct rule. The provinces in the Near East were like modules, frequently reassembled into some new empire but often essentially the same people in the same place as before. The rulers of the Two Rivers did however use a devastating method of political control, copied by Joseph Stalin in the 20th century; this was the wholesale relocation of tribes to some other part of their Empire.

One example of this was to affect the developing young nation of Israel, with lasting consequences. In fact, the Jewish Bible story of Jonah is the first place many people will hear about the Assyrians. The people of Nineveh repented of their sins and came back to God, following the coming of Jonah, who preached to them. Nineveh is present-day Mosul, the original town of the Assyrian nation, founded c.5000 BC.

In the 13th century BC, according to the Bible, Moses led the

Israelites, who had come from outside Egypt, from Egypt to Canaan, where they settled, probably in quite limited numbers, as there was no King of Israel so far and it has proved difficult to find historical records of the event outside the Bible itself. Canaan is the narrow fertile strip bordering the sea which now comprises Israel, Palestine, Lebanon and western Syria. A group of people called the *Hibiru* are mentioned in literary sources but the idea that they were Hebrews is only one of a number of viable explanations. Maybe they were, maybe they weren't. We are on more certain ground around 1000 BC, when King David created the Kingdom of Israel. The Books of Samuel, Kings and Chronicles give us more information about Israel than we have about any other Iron Age Kingdom in the Levant[84]. Over two centuries later, "the Assyrian came down like a wolf on the fold."[85]

In 734 BC King Tiglath-Pileser III invaded the region of Palestine and in 733 Assyria took large swathes of land from Israel. In 724 BC Shalmaneser V marched against Hoshea of Israel. In 721 BC the Northern Kingdom of Israel was destroyed by Assyria and the refugees fled to the southern kingdom of Judea, which paid tribute to the Assyrians, implying a subject nation status. In 701 BC King Sennacherib of Assyria led a military campaign, conquering the coastal cities of the land of Israel, and was thus immortalized at 2 Kings and 2 Chronicles and later by Lord Byron.

In 612 BC the New Babylonian Empire arose and wrested territory from Assyria. By 609 BC Assyria had lost control of her western outpost Harran and her last political significance. (The Babylonians in turn were to fall prey to the Persians and then Alexander of Macedon.) In 586 BC the Babylonian King called Nebuchadnezzar in the Bible conquered Jerusalem, destroyed Solomon's Temple and deported the people of Judah to Babylon. During this period, known as the Exile or Captivity, the Prophet Ezekiel had religious visions, which were to become the basis of much early Jewish mysticism. The entire center of gravity of the Jewish world moved from Jerusalem to Mesopotamia, because of the Babylonian conquest. Religious commentaries, called the Talmud, were written in Babylonia, and the anguish of the Jewish Diaspora and subjugation is echoed in the Christian Book known as Revelation, whose Jewish Christian author rails against the "Great Whore of Babylon" in this precise context of cultural dislocation and conquest. A very great deal of the Bible is concerned with this episode, which echoes the earlier tribulations of Moses and the early Israelites in Egypt under Pharaoh.

In the period around 539 BC the Judeans returned to Jerusalem and started to build Zerubbabel's Temple. The Persians and then the Greeks conquered the Near East. In 323 BC Alexander the Great died and his empire, including Israel, was carved up between regional overlords. In 166 BC the Maccabees revolted and Israel enjoyed another rare period of independence. In 63 BC the Romans conquered Israel and in 6 BC we have the probable birth date of Jesus, or Yeshua Bar Yusef.

There is a tradition to explain the early conversion of the Assyrians to Christianity[86]. King Abgar V Ukomo of Osroene in Assyria became very ill. Nobody could help him. Help was sought from the famous healer Jesus, in Jerusalem, and the courier Hannan asked him to come and heal the King. Jesus, who knew his days were numbered at that time, is said to have replied:

"…And that you have written to me that I should come to you – for that which I have been sent here is now fulfilled, and I am about to ascend to my Father who sent me, and when I have ascended to him, I will send you one of my disciples, who will heal and cure whatever pain you have, and all who are with you he will lead to eternal life. Your city will be blessed, and no enemy in the future will ever take it over."

Either St. Thomas or St Mor Adai went to Assyria, and successfully cured the King, whereupon the entire Assyrian people were converted to Christianity.

The Assyrians had only two religions, the state religion of Ashurism and Christianity. They never converted to Islam. Ashurism lasted until the 3rd century AD. It is perhaps not surprising that they were the first nation to convert to Christianity. They had a Holy Trinity already, and elements of the Jewish faith were derived from their own. These people were later a Christian bulwark against Islam. They sent missionaries to India, Japan, the Philippines and throughout Asia, even as far as Peking in around 86 AD, so that Marco Polo was astonished to find Christians already at the Imperial Court of China when he arrived. They gave their Assyrian (Aramaic) alphabet to the Mongol Tartars when they first adopted literacy. The Assyrian Christians were decimated by the Muslims. Only a few million survive. There are five different denominations in the modern Assyrian Church, which still uses Aramaic. The terrible Assyrian holocaust, beginning in 1918, saw nearly two-thirds of the Assyrian Christians massacred at the hands of the Muslims and Kurds. Further troubles broke out in 2003 with the fall of Saddam Hussein.

There are websites set up to preserve Assyrian culture, and you can learn their Aramaic script and language online. If you look at translations of the Dead Sea Scrolls, some are written in Hebrew but others in Aramaic. The Aramaic alphabet is very close to Hebrew. Aramaic is still in use among contemporary Assyrians and a derivative of it is used by the Mandaeans or Baptizers, who honor St John the Baptist, found among the so-called Marsh Arabs of southern Iraq, who are also scattered and diminished as a result of persecution.

The Assyrians, then, were succeeded first by the Babylonians, but only briefly. Nabonidus[87], the last king of the neo-Babylonian Empire (who reigned 556 to 539 BC), had on his stela (on display at the British Museum) the holy trinity of Sun, Moon and Venus, but he preferred Sin the Moon to the other two. This comes first in sequence and is clearly larger than the other two symbols, to stress its importance. The winged disc here is thought to be the Sun rather than Ashur (he was, after all, not an Assyrian). He was the son of Sin's priestess at Harran. He tried to abolish the worship of the other gods to the horror of his subjects. They thought he was mad.

When the Persians invaded, Nabonidus was punished and Babylon was independent no more. In time the fertile plains which had been overwatered by too many irrigation canals started to become too salty and turned to barren desert. The city walls of mighty Babylon became the boundary of a game reserve for hunting animals. The other cities became mounds or tells, haunted (poetically speaking) by Djinn, preserving ziggurats and palaces for the explorers of modern times. The languages of these peoples were lost for over 1,000 years.

But a once nomadic people who once paid tribute to an Assyrian King lived on. They were the Hebrews. They preserved the ancient astrology in the Dead Sea scroll records and their wisdom teachers may have remembered the Tree of Life diagram from the Royal Palaces of Assyria.

Based on the story in Exodus, Jewish families kept a menorah or multi-branched candlestick which is simply a very stylised Tree of Life as explained by numerous books on Kabbalah. Note that it is designed with nodal points, as was the Assyrian Tree of Life. A useful diagram[88] in Zev ben Shimon Halevi's book *Kabbalah* shows the middle pillar as the central branch or trunk, with the side sephiroth on the side pillars (although modern explanations attribute it to the seven days of creation or the seven days of the week, which are of course routinely named after planetary gods). The fundamental concept is a number of natural lights, so oil was replaced by candles in modern times but electrical lights meet with rabbinical disapproval. I am of course aware of the 9 branched candlesticks used at Hanukkah but that seems to be a later development, based on the events of the Maccabees period.

The lights might remind us of the seven ancient planets. I have also discovered that there was a cult of seven lights among the Kurds, who are descendants of the ancient Hurrians, and have for thousands of years lived around the mountains to the north of Mesopotamia and sometimes settled in the plains as well.

It is a little known fact that the Kurds had a Jewish Royal Family in the 1st millennium AD[89]. The Talmud holds that Jewish deportees were settled in Kurdistan 2,800 years ago by the Assyrian King Shalmaneser III (reigned 858-824 BC). By the early 5th century the Kurdish royal house of Adiabene had converted from Judaism to Christianity. Both Kurdish Christians and Jews used Aramaic for their records, which were kept at their capital of Arbela (modern Arbil). Jews were, very unusually, allowed by their rabbis to proselytise among the Kurds, with the result that Kurdish beliefs are influenced more by Judaism than by Christianity. (Kurdish Jews in the 17th century ordained the world's first woman rabbi, Rabbi Asenath Barzani.) Therefore there is considerable material to suggest that the influence may have flowed two ways. The cult of seven angels[90] is a feature of the astrological traditions of this whole region. In appendix two, I have summarized what I know of the cult of seven angels and its influence upon neighboring cultures.

Around 100 AD there arose a type of Jewish mysticism called *Merkavah* or Riders of the Chariot. These people had studied Ezekiel's visions and had a method of ascending spiritually to heaven through seven palaces, for which passwords had to be given, and great purity was required to avoid peril. The "palaces" are precursors of the sephiroth. I cannot prove the interesting possibility that these palaces also correspond to the chakras of yoga but neither can I disprove that theory. As Kabbalists have for a long time drawn correlations between the human body and the Sacred Tree, it is entirely possible. These "palaces" appear to pre-date the chakras of yoga by around 6 centuries, if the extant literary sources are a reliable indicator. Anyone who wishes to consider the question of body/spirit correlations in Jewish mysticism still further would be well advised to read the Sepher Yetzirah (Book of Formation), a short but dense text which was written down around 200 AD. The commentary on that book of Rabbi Aryeh Kaplan is unsurpassed in brilliance[91]. Paramahansa Yogananda, the author of that *tour de force* the *Autobiography of a Yogi*, wrote of a connection between the chakras and the seven palaces[92] mentioned in *Revelation*. Perhaps the Jewish mystics invented the chakras?

In the 11th century this Jewish mystical tradition was first named Kabbalah, by the Spanish mystic, Solomon Ibn Gabriol. In the 12th century a major text called the Bahir was published. Around the end of that century there appeared the best known text, the Zohar (Book of Splendour) attributed to Moshe De Leon as either author or compiler. In 1290 a little known Jewish text, the *Shaare Orah*, was written by his friend, the Castilian Rabbi Yosef Gikatila, who was 8 years younger than De Leon. It was later translated into Latin as *Portae Lucis* or Gates of Light. In 1516, this Latin version was to be the first known book ever illustrated by the Sephirothic Tree diagram.

Today in Los Angeles the Kabbalah Centre teaches a new form of the ancient lore to its film stars and singers. These are our modern heroes and heroines. As a film of *The Epic of Gilgamesh*, the hero of Uruk, is in production at the time of writing, I marvel at the continuity of tradition.

Appendix 1: Shiva

Lord Shiva is the God of the Yogis. Some sources say that he was a real human person who later became divine or realised divinity. Shiva is part of the "Holy Trinity" of Hindu religion. Brahma is the Creator, Vishnu the Preserver and Shiva the Destroyer. This is not destroyer in any sinister sense but rather destruction of karma and illusion. The path of the yogi is a gradual but disciplined journey towards these goals. (See for, example, *"Autobiography of a Yogi"* by the late Paramahansa Yogananda (1893-1952), widely rated as one of the most extraordinary books ever published on human spiritual life.) Karma means actions and the fruits of actions. The illusions (admirably summarized by Alan Watts in *"The Taboo Against Knowing Who You Are"*)[93] involve the ego imagining that it is separate, a misconception that arises from ignorance and merely superficial examination of the human situation.

Investigation reveals repeatedly that all boundaries are very porous. Maya or the world of illusion misleads us but we have to live in it. The classic methods of the yogi include the mental techniques of Raja Yoga, the concentration of Mantra Yoga, the religious devotion of Bhakti Yoga and the service of Karma Yoga. The range of human temperaments is catered for admirably.

The early version of Shiva is portrayed in Indus Valley art as Shiva Pasupati or Lord of the Animals[94]. It depicts Lord Shiva, surrounded by animals, wearing antlers and sitting in the yogic Lotus pose. Each antler has seven tines or prongs on each side, making 28 tines in all, which is a lunar month correspondence.

The so-called Celtic artefact, the Gundestrup cauldron[95], an illustrated large silver cup found in a Danish bog, is not in fact Celtic in conception but an uncomprehending copy of original Indian Tantric designs with Shiva Pasupati, not Cernunnos, as the central figure. The European artists of the Cauldron, possibly

Thracians, had never seen the Indian animals they portrayed but did notice a similarity between Shiva and Cernunnos, probably because of an already ancient connection through a common Indo-European or Aryan language family (note that the word Aryan is cognate with both "Iran" and the adjectival form of the Irish name for Ireland, "Eireanne"). A fully detailed analysis of the Cauldron designs would require a separate book.

One curious feature of the Cauldron design is that Shiva sits in the Lotus asana (yoga posture) holding a ram-headed snake. Shiva in India is the God of the Yogis and holds a snake ("raising the snake"?). The cobra is frequently used in yogic art to represent the fiery serpent energy or kundalini or Shakti, said to reside at the base of the spine. The object of so-called kundalini yoga is to release and safely raise this energy up the spine until it envelopes the crown. This may be shown as the cobra over the head of the yogi, with its head fully extended. The cheeks of the cobra come out to form an overall impression of a hood but the face of the ram is in fact rather similar to that of the cobra, if you allow for scale. The hood could be misinterpreted as a ram's neck. If you compare the "ram headed serpent" with the yogic cobra, it is hard to resist the conclusion that one was copied from the other by someone unfamiliar with Indian wildlife[96].

The journey of the kundalini serpent up the spinal channel is not a phenomenon restricted to enthusiastic yogis. It is a project best undertaken slowly and carefully under guidance. I have read accounts on websites of individuals who had "involuntary" kundalini experiences which caused them great surprise and distress. There is a feeling of heat and pressure in the head, and perhaps of an energy flow going upwards, making it hard to sleep. Essentially this is likely when the subject has no training in how to control the experience and I have found that there are even schools of yoga which regard the whole subject as dangerous and do not teach it. The problem with failing to teach kundalini is that it is also a failure to teach the safety mechanisms. It is difficult for the victims of involuntary kundalini arousal to find psychologists who understand what is happening to them and the result is that they may be trapped in a prolonged and disturbing shock to their nervous system. Without training and purification, there may not be the capacity to cope easily with the increased level of energy.

However, the energy can stop and any yogis who are adequately trained can give simple techniques to calm it. (All of these phenomena point to the existence of an "energy body" with "energy centres".) The core concept of the "cure" for kundalini is that of reversing flow. Therefore one might stand and stroke an arm *downwards* with the other arm repeatedly, and slowly, and alternately, to ground or earth the energy flow. Also the breath should be consciously slowed as much as possible. The energy flows best when the energy centres are whipped up into a state of excitement (for example, the whirling of Dervishes to achieve a mystical state; they practice a yogic rite identical to the first of the rejuvenating posture series popularly known as "The Five Tibetans")[97]. Therefore the last thing you should do when trying to "cure" kundalini arousal is to do vigorous physical exercise. In a nutshell, "slow down".

Scientific investigation of kundalini phenomena is patchy. One of the most suggestive projects was undertaken by a Japanese scientist, Dr Hiroshi Motoyama[98], whose book *Theories of the Chakras: Bridge to Higher Consciousness* is an account of how his personal experience of this force led him to research a connection with the subtle body channels of acupuncture. It seems that there is a link between the Indian *nadis* (channels) and Chinese/Japanese *meridians*.

Another aspect of this force is the location of the energy centers in the human body. All that I have read about attempts to link it to hard physical science suggest that the endocrine system of glands which regulate the human body *provide the physical locus for the nodes of the energy vortices or wheels of the chakras*. Yogic techniques aimed at rejuvenation and healing that I have investigated appear to be based on the facts that (a) the spine contracts as we get older and (b) upper endocrine glands start to fail as we get older, e.g. the thymus declines in our twenties. These endocrine glands are part of our immune system. I have seen health websites (not related to yoga) attempting to sell thymus product, and I recommend readers to avoid it, as it comes from cows. A free Taoist technique (from China) for boosting energy involves daily tapping with both fists on the chest over the thymus. Yoga techniques for boosting health include spinal stretches and stimulation of the upper body glands/chakras by certain repeated movements. Do not practice any of these techniques without a suitably qualified teacher.

Is there a connection between the chakras and the nodes on the Assyrian Tree of Life? Many modern books on both Kabbalah and Yoga have attempted to draw a parallel with the Kabbalistic Tree. The classic correlation is between the Middle Pillar and the central channel or Sushumna Nadi and the two outer pillars with the channels known as Ida and Pingala. These channels feature in nostril breathing or Pranayama. Breath meditation and indeed many other kinds of meditation were also practiced by the early Kabbalists (see *Meditation and the Kabbalah* by Rabbi Aryeh Kaplan[99].)

It is very noticeable that the Crown (Kether) is at the summit of both systems. The Assyrian drawing of the winged god (arguably Ashur) above the Tree is very suggestive of the Sahasrara Padma or Thousand Petalled Lotus of Cosmic Consciousness or Shiva Consciousness. Since there is no helpful accompanying text by the Assyrian designer, I cannot know if this is coincidence or not.

There are of course 7 major chakras and 10 sephiroth but, as many of the sephiroth come in pairs, it is quite possible to treat each pair as equivalent to one major chakra. Readers should be cautious here as the chakra concept is possibly not ancient. The earliest literary references to multiple chakras occur relatively late and mention less than seven centres[100]. Indian literary sources are quite inconsistent about the number of chakras. (But see Yogananda, *op. cit.*, at p.184, who argues that the chakras are the seven stars or churches at *Revelation* 1:20.)

Where I find it hardest to correlate the two systems is in modern details such as the color correspondences and so on. Clearly too much history of separate development has taken place to join them easily nowadays.

Another approach which is interesting is to relate the Tree to the Tao; a book[101] on that subject by Eric Yudelove, called *The Tao and the Tree of Life,* is recommended for further study. I am convinced that Taoism is strongly influenced by Hindu tantra and yoga traditions but that in adapting the tradition the Chinese stripped away the religious aspects to make this primarily a medical/martial arts system. Long life may indeed often be a by-product of a successful practice of yoga but to the Chinese that was an end in itself. Yudelove would be stretching across a linking system to join two others that fall geographically on either side. The systems originating to the west of China were clearly religious in the sense of having god characteristics within the mainstream tradition. The dualism of Yin/Yang is a hidden potential in the triadic structures of the Tree that becomes more obvious in the Shiva/Shakti dualism of Tantra and finally dominates in the Chinese way of the Tao. The real dualism in the Tree is expressed not only in the two outer pillars (especially in the sephirothic pair Chokmah/Binah) but also between Kether and Malkuth.

Appendix 2: The Kurdish Cult of Angels or Cult of Seven[102]

The Kurds of Western Asia are mostly Sunni Muslims and there are also around half a million Shiite Kurds. However, there are many other religious traditions in this region.

The Hurrians (or Mitanni) are the main ancestors of the modern Kurds, certainly of those who are not in the ruling class, which appears to be Indo-European. They have lived in approximately the same region since the beginning of recorded history and are a different people from the Assyrians.

The modern Kurds are found mainly in south-east Turkey and Northern Iraq (in the Kurdish Autonomous Region) and some neighbouring countries; but of course refugees are found in many other countries. The modern Kurdish language is, like Farsi, a Persian language of the Eastern Indo-European branch.

In the Crusades, the great leader of the Arabs, Saladin, was a Kurd. His people were famed for their fighting prowess. The Kurds are one of the most persecuted peoples in the Near East. They were promised their own state by a Treaty made in the early 20th century but the great powers were not favourably impressed by their tendency to revolt and so the opportunity passed. It is difficult to see what the boundaries of such a state would be as the land, shaped today like an inverted "V", straddles inhospitable mountains and it could easily be landlocked. That is a matter for politicians.

For information on the Hurrians I turned to writings of Piotr Bienkowski[103], Curator of Egyptian and Near Eastern Antiquities at the National Museums and Galleries on Merseyside and Honorary Research Fellow at the University of Liverpool, the author of many books and papers on the archaeology and culture of the ancient Near East and Egypt. He states that the Hurrians were an ethnic group present in the ancient

Near East from the third to the first millennia BC, whose kingdom of Mitanni became one of the great powers rivalling Egypt and Hatti. The key to the language is one of the Amarna letters written by Tushratta of Mitanni to Amenophis of Egypt. Hurrian is non Indo-European.

The Hurrians spoke an obscure language related only to Urartian (an otherwise unique language spoken near Mount Ararat in Turkey and not to be confused with *Ugaritic* which was a North-West Semitic language closely related to Hebrew and Aramaic, among others). The Urartian state was a confederation of Hurrian tribes around Lake Van and Mount Ararat, founded in the 9th century BC.

Bienkowski describes Mitanni as a powerful Hurrian state in North Mesopotamia and Syria. The core of Mitanni was the Khabur Valley (a tributary of the Euphrates with a source in the mountainous region of south-east or Kurdish Turkey) and its capital Washshukanni must have been located there although it is not yet positively identified. By the mid-fifteenth century BC, Mitanni had conquered the kingdoms of Aleppo, Assyria, Nuzi, Alalakh and Kizzuwatna, and stretched to the Mediterranean Sea. Its kings campaigned against Egypt and Hatti. The peace treaty with Egypt was confirmed by a series of diplomatic marriages. Tushratta of Mitanni twice sent the statue of Ishtar of Nineveh to Egypt to help heal the pharaoh. Mitanni was eventually annexed by the Assyrian King Shalmaneser I (c.1274-1244 BC).

Intriguingly for historians of the lens and telescope, Bienkowski states that, "it has been argued that the expansion of glass production in the fifteenth or fourteenth century BC should be attributed to Mitanni, and the best early glass comes from Nuzi, but *the correlation of glass innovation with the Hurrians has not been proved.* (From which I infer that it has not been disproved, either. IF)

Nuzi (also known as Yorgan Tepa) was a town located in

North-Eastern Iraq. Its importance can be gauged from the finding there of *a palace with over 100 rooms and courts, a drainage system, bathrooms and toilets, marble paving and wall paintings influenced by Egyptian and Aegean designs.* These astonishing trappings of luxury come from the 2nd millennium BC, long before the Roman Empire. The evidence points to trade and travel as far as Greece and Egypt. The destruction and looting of Nuzi are normally attributed to the Assyrians.

Bienkowski states that Hurrian social, economic and religious practices are best attested in the archives from Nuzi, which had a predominantly Hurrian population. It appears that the Hurrians were ruled by an Indo-European military aristocracy, skilled in the use of chariots. This elite were known as the *maryannu* which probably means young man or warrior. Much of the Hurrian religion was taken over by the Hittites, including their chief deity, the weather god Teshup.

Teshup was a storm god who became head of the Hittite pantheon during the New Kingdom (from 1400 BC) and was known as Tishpak in Mesopotamia, where he was also worshipped, as well as in Syria and Anatolia. His epithet was "king of heaven". He was depicted carrying a mace, axe or trident, sometimes a bolt of lightning, and wearing a sword. His sacred animal was the bull. (Note this was also the sacred animal in Mithraism, which derived from some interplay between the Hurrian religion and Zoroastrianism, and in the cults of Poseidon and Shiva, both of whom carried a trident. The Mesopotamian storm god Adad or Hadad also had a bull connection since the clouds were called his "bull-calves" – IF.) There was a cult and temple of Teshup at Nuzi.

Other Hurrian gods were adopted from the Mesopotamian pantheon. An important part of their religious practices were magical rituals accompanied by incantations. (This sounds like the practices of early wizards or magi –IF.)

Archaeologists would like to dig up the medieval city of

Harran in Turkey, close to the border with Syria[104]. This had a number of fascinating planetary temples and was an ancient centre of the Moon cult, with its crescent symbol well known from Mesopotamian stelae. The crescent moon was adopted in Byzantium as a symbol and later became a well known symbol all over again throughout the Near East. Although usually counted as a Mesopotamian outpost, home of the **Sabian cult** who nurtured the Hermetic writings, it is noticeable that it lies within Kurdish/Hurrian heartlands.

The native Hurrian/Kurdish religion is known by scholars as the **Cult of Angels** or Yazdnism. As there were seven good angels and seven bad ones, I tend to abbreviate this to the Cult of Seven. The religion is behind a number of better known ones. I first discovered aspects of this religion when reading[105] G I Gurdjieff's *"Meetings with Remarkable Men"*. This 20th century "rascal guru" explored the Middle East looking for teachers of the ancient wisdom traditions and found the **Yezidis**, who I now understand to be a branch of the Cult of Angels.

There are certainly many faiths in the region. It is striking how often these faiths have adapted to the arrival of Islam only to find there is a dispute about whether they are really Islamic or not. (There is an obvious parallel in Christianity, whose Christmas trees and Easter eggs and bunnies have no Biblical authority or precedent whatsoever but have the huge attraction of great charm and tradition.)

The central concept of the Cult of Angels is that the Creator left the world alone and it is administered by 7 angels over 7 epochs. These angels are ethereal beings of light. They have counterparts, 7 dark angels of matter. The cult has a number of branches including the **Yazdans** but the cult's best known branch is the **Yezidis**, who worship a Peacock[106]. These people constitute less than 5% of the Kurdish population. The Yezidis have four major annual celebrations including the Jam and the feast of Yezid. **Yazdanism** or the Cult of Angels is a variation of the

Kurdish name of the Yezidism branch. Yazdanism was the name of the entire religion before it fragmented but before that it may have been named after the Haq, its eternal, all-encompassing deity, the Universal Spirit.

Later religions which manifested these beliefs include **Manichaeism, Gnosticism, Mithraism,** and in the modern world, **Baha'ism.** The **Babis** believed in the transmigration of the soul, as do followers of the Cult of Angels. They did not mourn the dead, as they believed the soul of a dead Babi, after spending a few days in a transitional stage, enters the body of another Babi, usually a newborn.

Akhenaten, the heretic Pharaoh who first introduced monotheism to Ancient Egypt, married a Kurdish princess. I believe that this is the likely origin of his monotheism. Those who speculate that there is a close connection instead between his **Atenism** and Judaism overlook the fact that Judaism would not worship the solar disc or portray the deity by any image.

It seems that **Mithraism** was a very successful bid to take over European religion. It started in Turkey and spread westwards right across Europe, being particularly a favourite of the Roman soldiers. Examples of a Mithraic bull-slaying scene are displayed in the British Museum and the Museum of London. Astrology was clearly a very important aspect of Mithraism and the zodiac features often in this scene, which was the focus of worship. There were 7 grades of initiation in the Mithraic mysteries, each linked to a planet.

Scholar David Ulansey has suggested that the religion started in response to the discovery of precession of the equinoxes by Hipparchus in the 2nd century BC[107]. He notes that the animals displayed in the conventional bull-slaying scene relate to the constellations on the celestial equator in the Age of Taurus. This would make Mithraism the first "New Age" religion. There can be no belief in "Astrological Ages" without a prior awareness of the precession of the equinoxes, i.e. the very slow progression around the zodiac band of the rising sign at the equinox. Any resolution of the debates about the real meaning of that religion is hampered by the lack of a sacred book of Mithraism, which is also a problem when studying the Ashur cult of Assyria.

Mithraism indisputably emerged from the matrix of Persian **Zoroastrianism,** since Mithras is a deity in that cult. However, Zoroastrianism itself appears greatly indebted to the Cult of Angels. It is dualistic and involves fire worship. (Note that the Zoroastrian symbol of the god in the winged disc resembles the symbol of Ashur, which is another argument for monotheism in Assyrian religious thought. It is likely that the symbol was taken directly from Ashurism.)

Mithraism had significant influence over the subsequent organisation of Christian worship, which clearly differs from Jewish practice in many respects. This may be because Mithraism was technically one of the Mystery religions, popular before and during the Roman Empire, which promised immortality to the initiated alone, as a result of secret rites. The concept of being saved by accepting a divine saviour, with a rite of passage to mark a new life, pre-dates Christian practice and is clearly not found within Judaism. Other Mystery religions included the rites of newcomer wine-god Dionysus (whose origins lie in the Near East but are mysterious since wine has been found in the Iranian village of Hajji Firuz dating to 6000 BC), Isis (the personification of the royal throne from Hellenistic Egypt) and Demeter (the Earth Mother from Greece). Where Christianity differed radically from other Mystery religions was that it offered admission to all, including both genders (unlike Mithraism), all races and all classes (including slaves). After the mass crucifixion of the slaves led by Spartacus, it is not hard to understand the apparent danger for the Romans of another cult of a crucified rebel.

If you wonder where the Kurds were on the map then, look at any map of the Roman Empire and examine Turkey, then known as Asia Minor to distinguish it from Greater Asia which lay beyond. The Romans divided it among many different nations. The Galatians, in the centre, were fierce Celtic-speaking invaders from Europe, who retained their language until the 5th century AD; but many of the other tribes, particularly those in the east, were simply various types of Kurd or Hurrian. The Kurdish provinces included Cappadocia, Cilicia and Commagene, for example.

The modern religion of the **Alevi Kurds** in Turkey is a manifestation of the Cult of Angels. Their practices include celebrating the New Year (Newroz) at the Spring Equinox, which identifies them as culturally Persian to the Turks. Both the Persians and the ancient Babylonians celebrated a great festival, lasting over a week, at the Spring Equinox.

The Alevi Kurds like to tie offerings to trees. I find the worship of the tree very suggestive of the artistic tradition in Assyria which is the main focus of this book.

A majority of the Dimila Kurds of Anatolia and some of their Kurmanji speaking neighbours follow this creed. They believe in Ali as the most important primary avatar of the Universal Spirit; he was the first Shiite Muslim Imam. Nevertheless, the theology of the Alevi Kurds contradicts the Koran. Alevis constitute about 20% of all Kurds.

The **Druze** of Lebanon are another regional religious group whose Islamic identity is questioned. They believe in reincarnation and a religion of light.

Sufism is also concentrated in this region. It has mystical practices which pre-date Islam and its leaders are called Shaikhs or Shaykhs, who might roughly equate to the guru. An overwhelming majority of both Muslim and non-Muslim Kurds are followers of one of the Sufi orders or tariqa. There are numerous Sufi Orders throughout the modern world. Some are avowedly Islamic and see themselves as practicing the inner, mystical aspect of the exoteric faith. Others distance themselves from Islam. The focus is on understanding that everything is an interaction with the Divine, whose nature is Love.

The whirling **Dervishes** of Turkey are a related group. Their aim is clearly to achieve mystic union with the divine through dance. I have spoken to somebody who saw this performed in Turkey. The dancers start whirling out of sight and by the time they appear in public they are in full trance. The long skirts are used so that they know when they are moving too close to another Dervish. The whirling dance continues for hours.

Yarsanism is centred deep inside the Guran region at Gahwara, 40 miles west of Kirmashan. These followers are found in one large concentration in Southern Kurdistan and many lesser centers in the Alburz mountains, Azerbaijan and Iraq.

The belief in angels is of course widespread through all the present day religions of the Book: **Judaism, Christianity and Islam**. It has also become a New Age phenomenon, as channels and mediums have claimed contact from angelic intelligences. Magicians of earlier eras, such as Dr John Dee, claimed to have communication with angelic intelligences; a direct contact made without priestly intermediary.

The working class Kurds have tended to avoid literacy; this trait has made scholarly study of their traditions rather difficult. However, there is an unbroken tradition going back over 4,000 years among these people and I am grateful for any records and insights that emerge.

Appendix 3: Shamanism and Kabbalah

The world of the shaman is often overlooked in surveys of Kabbalah but it is essential for establishing the full historical context and provenance. In the 20th century a Romanian intellectual came to Paris and Chicago and wrote lucid, brilliant, definitive works on little understood spiritual topics such as shamanism and yoga. His name was Mircea Eliade. He is renowned as the first author to publish a clear overview of shamanism[108]. The Asiatic shaman is the earliest *religious* figure known in human society, the priest of the Stone Age and earlier, if you like.

The role of the shaman is complex, involving healing, trance, spirit journeys, finding lost souls and the achievement of ecstasy. Common elements between shamanism and Kabbalah include initiations, ascension to other worlds or planes, seeking of divine beings, healing practices and use of the sacred Tree and particularly a Tree of Life or Immortality. Many Asiatic shamans lived in a hut supported by a central pole; this was regarded as a symbol of the Cosmic Tree and offerings were laid at its base. Some tribes set up shamanic trees or posts with notches outside their homes. The Tree has multiple meanings for the shaman; it is the world axis, and the Universe in constant regeneration but also it symbolizes the sky or planetary heavens. The latter function was very important in Siberian and Central Asian shamanism.

Often the Tree is imagined as having a Bird at the top and a Snake at its roots, imagery which recurs in world mythology. Mystical numbers occur in this context. The most common numbers in shamanism are 7 and 9. It is thought that originally there were 3 worlds in shamanism and that 9 may be derived from the square of 3, while the 7 derive from the traditional planets plus moon and Sun. A tribe called the Vogul believed that heaven was reached by climbing a stairway of 7 stairs.

The three worlds consist of an upper world (sky), middle world (humans) and underworld. Obviously this symbolism is very long-lived, featuring in European mythology and elsewhere, and still recognisable in the modern world (e.g. Tolkien's "Middle Earth"). Various Asiatic tribes had shamanic posts or trees with 7 or 9 notches to climb. There are said to be 7 or 9 heavens inhabited by 7 or 9 gods, in certain tribes. There are certainly examples of Trees with 7 branches and this is a symbol best known today as the Menorah or stylised branched candle-holder used in Jewish religious households. It was not only trees but also sacred poles and mountains with four sides (pyramids) which were seen as the central axis.

Asiatic shamanism and its African equivalent lie at the roots of the religions that developed respectively in the urban cultures of Ancient Iraq and Ancient Egypt. This context helps us to understand, for example, the reason for building pyramids. The Tree of Life symbol (with 9 stages) was clearly used by the Assyrian people of Northern Iraq as numerous images found by archaeologists attest; also the cosmic number 7 was central to the ancestral religion of the Kurdish people who were and are their northern neighbors.

Appendix 4: The British Museum and Louvre Exhibits

The Museum offers daily tours of the Ancient Near East exhibits. The website is www.thebritishmuseum.ac.uk

The most relevant rooms in the British Museum are currently as follows:

Lower Floors
Ancient Near East: 88, 88a and 89.

Main Floor
*Ancient Near East: 6, 7, 8, 9, 10 (room 7 includes numerous Assyrian palace reliefs of Sacred Trees – displayed reliefs collected from palaces at Nimrud, Nineveh and Khorsabad)
The Great Court: stela with god symbols
1: case 20 has inscribed objects of Dr John Dee, showing continuity of tradition regarding Enoch, angels and the four quarters

Upper Floors
Asia: 67, turn left for Indian planetary god sculptures from astral temples, showing seated in yogic pose with mudras (esoteric hand gestures); the North and South Nodes of the moon's orbit are also represented, as implicated in eclipse omens
Ancient Near East: 53-56: includes reliefs of Gilgamesh, omen tablets and many other objects discussed in this book
Greece and Rome: 69 includes many deity figures discussed in this book

In the Louvre, Paris
The Ancient Near East: Room 4
Khorsabad, Capital of Sargon II.

Genie holding a poppy flower. Also, stylised Tree of Life, identified as a pine tree

From excavations of P.E.Botta, 1843-44, AO 19869.

Appendix 5: Leaves Of Life – Medical Use

Was there a real Tree of Life? Both the Old and New Testaments make many references to it. The New Testament identifies the Messiah with the Tree and uses the Tree symbolism of the Crucifixion – "Christ died on the Tree". Although my work has emphasised the date-palm, which dominates the Near East, I also found that for at least 6,000 years the olive tree (which dominates the Mediterranean region) has been called the Tree of Life. It is related to the ash, jasmine and lilac.

This interested me because in the Norse tradition the ash is known as the World Tree, Yggdrasil, which is a cosmic axis and ladder between the three worlds, rather like the Tree of Life. This seems to be a typically shamanic model of the universe and it has been noted that early Kabbalah (such as literature about the Riders of the Chariot, with the theme of ascension) appears to have shamanic roots.

Shamanism is the root religion of a vast swathe of native peoples, stretching from Europe through Asia to the Americas, characterised by a medicine man or shaman who experiences altered states of consciousness, travels in an alternate reality where spirit beings are seen, talks with gods and birds or animals and even plants, and causes healing to take place.

The Greek Goddess Athene planted the olive in Athens, in legend, among the rocks of the Acropolis. She reputedly gave it powers to illuminate the darkness, soothe wounds, restore libido, heal illness and provide nourishment.

Olive oil became a staple part of the healthy Mediterranean diet and a source of fuel. The leaves have many healing properties, some of which were known in ancient Arab textbooks, but others which medical research has brought to the fore only in the last two decades. Most notable is William R. Fredrickson's pioneering research and development of olive leaf extract as a treatment for infectious diseases.

The conditions which are claimed to respond to treatment include all viruses, all bacteria, even the antibiotic-resistant flesh eating bugs; fungal and yeast infections; and more.

Olive leaf extract combined in a drink with whole lemon, olive oil, and some other substances, has *reputedly* been demonstrated to have the ability to assist in changing some patients from HIV positive status to HIV negative. I do not wish to give false hope. I would refer anyone seeking advice to a medical practitioner in the first instance. For HIV a number of other treatments should be taken in conjunction and these are specified in Dr Morton Walker's book[109].

Olive leaf contains *protease inhibitors.*

In the 1970s research into calcium elenolate, found in olive leaf, proved that it could inactivate myxoviruses, which are the germs that cause flu types A, B and C. A special treatment (developed recently) is however required to enable the active substance to survive for more than minutes after ingestion.

Key points

- The olive is traditionally called the Tree of Life
- The olive was established at Athens in legend by the goddess Athene
- The olive was a major source of food and fuel for the Mediterranean
- The leaves are the source of powerful medical substances
- Olive leaf has been found valuable for viruses, bacteria, fungi and worm infections
- A special treatment is required to make the leaf remain effective after ingestion

Appendix 6: Enigma of the Jewish synagogue zodiacs[110]

Jewish religious law, equally familiar to Christians, prohibits the worship of other gods and prohibits the making of graven images. However, this rule is open to different interpretations, which is why Protestants have quarrelled with Catholics over the imagery in their churches and cathedrals.

In Jewish synagogues there are sometimes found zodiac diagrams. The zodiac design is also found in some Gothic cathedrals, which may be permitted as an acceptable portrayal of the calendar of the Church Year. Synagogues started to be built from the 1st century AD because the need arose. There was at any one time only one Temple in Jerusalem, which suffered periodic destruction, and in any case the Jews started to spread out further and further into the wider world. In fact they had already done this in the Babylonian Exile. At first they met in people's houses but later they needed special buildings.

The first synagogue did not have a zodiac. However, we know that from the 2nd century onwards many synagogues were built in Israel which included a zodiac wheel design, the center being filled with a figure in a chariot, normally designated as the Sun God Helios. This is a bizarre enigma, given the religious rules above. I wanted desperately to explain it to my own satisfaction.

I had the benefit of hearing a fascinating illustrated talk on the subject by archaeologist Roz Park in October 2004. She specialises in Egyptology and her dissertation was on the Denderah zodiac (Egypt, 1st century AD – exhibited at the Louvre, Paris). I am certainly not going to steal her thunder by publishing her most interesting original insights (which I very much hope she will do) but it is useful to outline here some of the remains that have been investigated. I badly needed to hear a good talk on the subject and I certainly received one.

The list of sites in Israel includes: Sepphoris (discovered 1993), Tiberias, Husifah, Beth Alpha, En Gedi, Rehob and Na'aran. Sepphoris is an early 5th century AD building. The synagogue used Greek and Hebrew. The zodiac design includes zodiac signs, months and four seasons. Each corner is filled with the bust of a woman. Rays of light emanate from the head of Helios in the centre of the zodiac wheel.

The synagogue at Tiberias (dated from 396-422 AD) shows Helios in the centre of the zodiac wheel, holding a globe representing the earth.

In the following days all sorts of wild and wonderful interpretations came to mind in a brain-storming session. These are mine and, if they are proved wrong, that is my responsibility entirely. It was only later that I started to read in an organized way on the subject. There are four different approaches which I considered in rapid succession. I apologize if some seem far-fetched but I believe it is useful to display the creative thought process, before I compare them with other views and try to reach a final evaluation.

Firstly, I started thinking about the Jewish and Babylonian calendar year. The month names are similar. I was thinking backwards from the medieval cathedrals and wondering if the zodiac helped worshippers to remember their festivals. The big problem with this is that the Jewish calendar is lunar and the zodiac is obviously solar.

Next, I thought about Queen Boudicca of the Iceni. Readers may at this point fear for my sanity or suspect a leg-pull. But I was thinking about a woman with streaming red hair standing in a chariot, putting the fear of God into the Romans. Was it possible that so was the artist? Was she so big an icon, that people at the far end of the Roman Empire would admire her in the following centuries? Well, Helios could have streaming red hair and this particular "Helios" might even be a woman, although it is generally assumed that this figure is male. What on earth would orthodox Jews want with this pagan British warrior-Queen? The only possible explanation was that they had mutual common enemies. If you look at my timeline, this period of Roman occupation entailed revolts that ended in vast slaughter by Roman soldiers, who just could not understand the alien ways of the conquered race. Both Celtic Britain and the Holy Land shared an identical seething hatred of oppressive rule by Romans, who just would not go away and leave them be. Both had royal lines whose supporters could not overcome the Emperor's legions. Boudicca's revolt was in 61 AD and the Jewish revolt in 66 AD, only 5 years apart. The Roman conquest of Britain was no secret. Roman authors such as Tacitus and Agricola published accounts which would have been read later throughout the Empire. So, yes, the Jews knew about Boadicea, the Roman name for Boudicca.

If Boadicea is passed off as Helios, the artist is trying to "pull a fast one" over the Roman soldiers, who might periodically inspect and check for signs of sedition. The familiar face of Helios Apollo would reassure them that the Jews were picking up "proper pagan Roman" ways. This interpretation is sarcastic and seditious. It still has the problem that it refers outside of the Jewish religious context. I could see that massive scepticism was a likely response.

My next speculation was more cautious. I was still interested in the idea of pulling a trick on the Romans but I thought more deeply about the Roman soldiers themselves. By this period they were mostly followers of the god Mithras, who was a solar hero. I was also thinking about "why synagogues"? New sacred buildings were springing up as new religions came to the fore. Firstly, Mithraism appeared in the 1st century BC in Asia Minor and spread throughout the Empire. Inside the Mithraeum, the worshipers faced a representation of Mithras, apparently slaying a bull, and a zodiac. The worshipers were initiated into seven grades, based on the traditional planets. So Mithraism is definitely an astral religion. Some of their artifacts are on display at the British Museum and the Museum of London, where you can check this for yourself. But Mithras was usually worshipped in a cave or crypt, not above ground.

Christian worship originated as a Jewish cult, meeting in people's houses, and then it attracted gentiles too and soon needed dedicated sacred buildings. These could not be called Temples, which sounded pagan, so they were called ecclesiae (churches), and they relate closely to the parallel development of the synagogue. Christian liturgy was rather new except that it borrowed heavily from Mithraic liturgy; in fact both were mystery religions worshipping a divine saviour. Just as Mithraism was the favoured cult of soldiers, Christianity was followed often by slaves, and, aside from its intrinsic virtues, this was partly due to its emphasis on equality, no doubt, but also perhaps because the great slave hero Spartacus and his followers faced crucifixion. So, the synagogue was a kind of church, for Jews, and the church was a kind of Mithraeum. If you wanted to fool the Roman soldiers, why not make the synagogue look like a familiar Mithraeum, with its zodiac? I was happier with this idea. The religious Jews could tell themselves that the sun god looked to the Romans like Mithras but they knew it was only an object in space so they weren't worshiping it.

Finally, I looked at Jewish mysticism, because I knew by now that I needed a Jewish cultural reference to make final sense of the "Helios" in the chariot. I found a correlation, a big one. This was the stage in Jewish mysticism when the practitioners were "Riders in the Chariot"! It could hardly be clearer! These mystics were following Ezekiel who lived in Babylonia. The zodiac clearly referred to the location of the Exile. The face in the chariot could be that of Ezekiel himself, transfigured as he rode up nearer to the Lord. Finally I had a possible Jewish religious explanation. And the Jewish Law on images was interpreted differently by different Rabbis, as ever.

Those were my initial thoughts. On reading widely, I discovered that many different theories had been put forward but the idea of a clear line separating Judaism and pagan astrology was simply not correct. Even Helios himself had a long history in Judaism. Texts and amulets from the period bear this out. Tradition taught that Abraham and his father Terah were astrologers and came from Babylonia, a region long renowned for its astrologers. There was also a rabbinical tradition that Moses had correlated the twelve signs to the twelve tribes of Israel or at least that this existed from antiquity. The early text Sepher Yetzirah was steeped in astrology and so were the Dead Sea scrolls, written shortly before the lifetime of Jesus and possibly collected by a Jewish community of mystics called the Essenes, who clearly venerated prophetic writings from both inside and outside the Torah. The Jews adopted the zodiac during the Babylonian exile, although it did not fit their calendar exactly. Zodiac signs were employed in Medieval illuminated prayer books, particularly of the Ashkenazi. In Eastern Europe, zodiacs also decorated synagogues built from the 17th to 20th centuries.

David Landau of Finland has argued that the Beth Alpha synagogue was not necessarily a synagogue and may have had no Jewish connection at all. He links it to Enochian writings. However, he has not extended his argument to the other buildings which I have listed, so we can assume for now that most of them were indeed synagogues.

Nearly all Jewish festivals take place at the full or new moon. "The nations reckon by the sun and Israel by the moon". Michael Avi-Yonah, a distinguished Israeli scholar, favours the calendar theory which I set out first. Others have considered the calendar theory and decided like me that the solar twelve-sign zodiacs do not give a calendar for use in the synagogues.

The next theory I read, propounded by E. E. Urbach and

others, was that the zodiacs were without any particular meaning. This did not square with their prominent positions.

E. R. Goodenough and others have postulated a cosmological meaning. They have tended to see Judaism as, in a sense, a Mystery religion, and the writings of Philo have been called in evidence. The average Jew was Hellenized, not sharing all the beliefs of the rabbis, and the inaccurate correlations of the zodiac mosaics showed that the details of practical astrology were unimportant to worshippers. The zodiac was a sign that God rules the world. He has a good deal of evidence but few supporters of the Jewish Mystery religion theory.

Perhaps the best way to see these Jewish zodiacs is to compare the medieval Christian ones. Both religions were monotheistic and saw the planets as powers or channels for the Supreme Being. The planets are part of the machinery of God's Universe, not his rivals. Jewish astrology is very ancient and one can still find rabbis who will write books in its defence, although many others would disagree with them.

It is also instructive to look at the continuation of Babylonian astrology and astronomy in the early phase of Islam, although later a firm view was taught that the Will of Allah always prevailed and one should not resort to astrologers. It was Islamic scholars who brought the astrolabe to Europe, where it became a valuable sky, space and time measuring instrument. I have attended a demonstration of how the two-dimensional astrolabe was used and understand that it is a flattened three-dimensional planisphere, which can be adjusted for every latitude by inserting spare plates stored in the underside compartment. Islamic believers were able to use the astrolabe to help them with their religious practices, such as finding the right time of day to pray and finding the direction of Mecca. In the 17th century the astrolabe was supplanted by the pendulum clock and the telescope.

Appendix 7: Was the Asherah of Canaan the Tree of Life?[111]

It is often asserted that the roots of Kabbalah lie in Egypt and/or Israel (ancient Canaan). This book establishes that is not the case. It is necessary to analyse the evidence for the other point of view in order to rebut it and strengthen the case for Assyria.

The "Egyptian origin" theory is mere speculation. Egypt was investigated by archaeologists earlier than Mesopotamia and is better known to the general public. However, there is nowadays no doubt that Mesopotamia was the cradle of Western civilization, which gave numerous important inventions to the world. It is precisely because of its close connection to us that Mesopotamia seems less exotic than Egypt.

Canaan

The Asherah (plural: *Asherim*) mentioned repeatedly in the Old Testament was a wooden pole set up near a grove of trees or in a high place, to honour a Canaanite Goddess. There are persuasive arguments that it was not itself a living tree. Canaan is the land on the eastern side of the Mediterranean, where the Israelites led by Moses settled, surrounded by other tribes. Asherah was the consort of El and the mother of the gods. The male god of the Canaanites, Baal, was also worshiped in pillar form.

Egypt ruled Canaan, Phoenicia and Syria around 1560-1200 BC. There is evidence to suggest that Egypt may have imposed its own pillar deities, Osiris and Hathor, on Canaan in this period. Osiris was a vegetation god, so it would not be surprising if he had a tree connection. In fact, the late myth of Osiris at Byblos finds him inside both a tree and a pillar.

Egypt

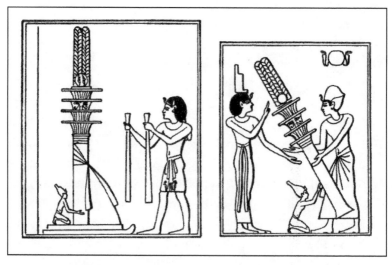

One of the common symbols of Osiris is the mysterious Djed pillar. This is often described as the spine of Osiris, on the strength of a sentence from the Book of the Dead and the resemblance to rib projections at the top and its horizontal banding. However, the human spine narrows towards the base to a point at the coccyx. A spine erected on the ground would simply fall over. I inspected a large Djed pillar in the Pharaoh Exhibition, while it was showing at the Museum of the Arab World in Paris. I noticed that it had a broad base, wider than the stem. This resembled a tree, not a spine. I deduced from this observation that the phrase in the Book of the Dead was metaphorical, like so much in Egyptian writing. Perhaps the author was saying that Osiris is *like* a spine. So is the trunk of a tree. That view means that the scribe was comparing the god with a tree, a very reasonable way of elucidating the nature of the vegetation god, since trees rule in the vegetable kingdom.

Hathor sometimes appears as a tree goddess, who offers cakes and drinks to the righteous dead. She was painted as emerging from the branches of a tree.

Conclusion

While I see a very interesting parallel there with Ishtar/Inanna, there is simply no evidence to support the idea that the specific stylised Tree of Life, with its sephiroth, found in either Assyrian or Jewish Kabbalah, came from these Canaanite/Egyptian sources. It is more likely that those were manifestations of the general belief in the usefulness of trees, in supporting civilization throughout the Near East.

It is even less likely that the Kabbalistic Tree of Life came from an Egyptian mystery source other than the cults of Osiris and Hathor.

Glossary

Assyria: the land in north-east Mesopotamia that is in present day Iraq; located in the fertile plains around the upper reaches of the River Tigris. The major cities included Ashur, Nineveh (adjacent to Mosul) and Nimrud (Kalhu, Biblical Calah). The land is ancient and was the centre of a major empire in parts of the 1st and 2nd millennium BC. It was always exposed to invasion from the mountains to the north and east and finally succumbed to the new Babylonian Empire. When that was replaced by the Persians and then the Greeks, it failed to reassert its ancient power. Both the Assyrians and Babylonians transported large numbers of captive Jews to their country, so that the world center of Jewry shifted eastwards to Mesopotamia. This meant that Mesopotamia had a very strong influence on the Jews from the 1st millennium BC onwards.

Chakras: wheels, energy vortices said to exist on central line of human body. Not detectable directly by science. Opinions vary as to number and location. Indian texts listing multiple chakras start to appear in 8th century AD.

Kundalini yoga (technically called Laya Yoga) seeks to raise energy safely up the line of chakras and requires prior purification. Each chakra has mantra and other correspondences.

Kabbalah: Jewish Mysticism. Now popular with Hollywood "personalities" but very ancient in origins. This book seeks to demonstrate that its roots lie in Assyria, before the foundation of Israel. As it is often an oral tradition, it is difficult to be certain of its date of origin using conventional scholastic methods; an intuitive approach is essential, so long as it does not conflict with scholastic findings.

Kurds: original inhabitants of the lands in eastern Anatolia (modern Turkey). They are referred to as Hurrians, Mitanni, Cappadocians and so on in ancient writings. At one stage they had a Jewish monarchy. Saladin was a Kurd. The mystic number 7 played an important part in their traditional religion. They have influenced the wider world in a way which is not widely known.

Mantra: a sacred word such as Om repeated silently or aloud in yogic spiritual practices.

Pythagoras: ancient Greek mystic and mathematician. Attributed various discoveries in geometry, number and so on which probably come from earlier Near Eastern and/or Druidic teachings. Some of his ideas resemble those of Kabbalists.

Sephirah: literally, number or counting. Plural: sephiroth. Hebrew term for an archetype or aspect of the Godhead. Used since ancient times in Kabbalah to locate and map a relative term in context on the schematic Tree of Life. Often ascribed numerous "correspondences" (linked concepts) in the same manner as the planets in astrology or the chakras in yoga.

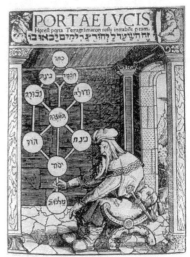

Sufism: major type of mysticism in the Islamic world. Has generated great works of poetry.

Tantra: a body of diverse writings and practices which forms an ancient and richly varied strand in Indian spiritual life. Veneration for a Great Goddess and Her consort Lord

Shiva are typical elements. Influence on yoga, Tibetan Buddhism is profound. Early Tantra was dominant in Indus Valley civilization (modern Pakistan). Later discouraged by Moghul and British conquerors. However, a British Judge writing as Sir Arthur Avalon was one of the first to bring its teachings to the West. The authentic tradition is plagued by misunderstandings and takes many years to study.

Tarot: set of illustrated cards originating in Northern Italy, no later than 1415 AD. A tributary of the River Po is named Taro. Said by some commentators to embody Hermetic or Gnostic ideals and does echo elements of the earlier Emerald Tablet of Hermes, a major alchemical text of extreme obscurity. Attempts to link to Sufis, ancient Egypt and Kabbalah may be unprovable. Mostly used for divination. Coincidence of 22 Major Trumps with number of Hebrew letters has led to much mapping onto the Tree of Life in modern times.

Select Bibliography

Addey, John; *Harmonics in Astrology* L. N. Fowler, London, 1976

Baigent, Michael; *From the Omens of Babylon: Astrology and Ancient Mesopotamia* Penguin Arkana, London, 1994

Bienkowski, Piotr and Millard, Alan (eds.); *Dictionary of the Ancient Near East* British Museum Press, London, 2000

Campion, Nicholas; *An Introduction to the History of Astrology* ISCWA, London, 1982

De Cleene, Marcel and Lejeune, Marie Claire; *Compendium of Symbolic and Ritual Plants in Europe, Vol.1* Man & Culture, Ghent, 2003

Ellis, Peter Berresford; *The Druids,* Constable, London, 1994 and *A Brief History of the Druids,* Robinson, London, 2002

Gleadow, Rupert; *Origins of the Zodiac* Jonathan Cape, London,1968

Halevi, Z; *Kabbalah* Thames & Hudson, London, 1979

Hopking, C.J.M.; *The Practical Kabbalah Guidebook* Godsfield Press, New York, 2001

Izady, M.R.; *The Kurds: A Concise Handbook* Taylor & Francis, London & Washington,1992

Kaplan, Aryeh; *Meditation and the Kabbalah* Weiser, York Beach, Maine, 1982

Kaplan, Aryeh; *Sepher Yetzirah* Weiser, York Beach, Maine, 1997

Kitson A. (ed.); *History and Astrology: Clio and Urania Confer* Mandala, London, 1989

Knight, Christopher and Lomas, Robert; *Uriel's Machine: the ancient origins of science* Arrow, London,1999

Lebeau R.; *Atlas des Hebreux* Editions Autremont, Paris, 2003

Motoyama, Hiroshi; *Theories of the Chakras: Bridge to Higher Consciousness* Quest Books, Wheaton, Illinois,1981

Opsopaus, John; *The Pythagorean Tarot* Llewellyn, St Pauls, MN, 2001 (Card deck and companion book)

Ponce C.; *Kabbalah,* Quest Books, Wheaton, Illinois,1973

Ridpath, Ian; *Star Tales* Lutterworth Press, Cambridge, 1988

Roaf, M.; *Cultural Atlas of Mesopotamia and the Ancient Near East,* Andromeda Oxford Limited, Oxford, 1990

Sandars, N.K. (trans.); *The Epic of Gilgamesh* Penguin Classics, London, revised 1972

Stone, Brian (trans.); *Sir Gawain and the Green Knight* Penguin Classics, London,1974

Temple, Robert; *The Crystal Sun – rediscovering a lost technology of the ancient world* Century, London, 2000

Walker, Dr. Morton; *Olive Leaf Extract* Kensington Books, New York,1997

Wise, Abegg & Cook; *The Dead Sea Scrolls* Harper San Francisco, 1996

Wolkstein, Diane and Kramer, Samuel Noah; *Inanna: Queen of Heaven and Earth; her stories and hymns from Sumer* Harper and Row, New York, 1983

Ulansey, David; *The Origins of the Mithraic Mysteries,* Oxford University Press, 1991

Yogananda, P.; *Autobiography of a Yogi,* Self-Realisation Fellowship, Los Angeles,1946

Yudelove, Eric Steven; *The Tao and the Tree of Life* Llewellyn, St Paul, MN, 1996

Printed Articles and Journals

Parpola, Simo; *The Assyrian Tree of Life: Tracing the origins of Jewish Monotheism and Greek Philosophy* Journal of Near Eastern Studies Vol. 52 No.2 (1993) University of Chicago, pp.161-298

Gnosis No.3 *"Kabbalah: Exploring the roots of mysticism",* ed. Jay Kinney, Meru Foundation, San Francisco,1988

Web Articles

The Pre-biblical Origins of the Baals and the Asherim as Egyptian

Pillar Gods and Goddesses Fused to Semitic Deities in Late Bronze Age Times (1560-1200 BCE) - Walter Reinhold Warttig Mattfeld y de la Torre, M.A. Ed.

The So-Called Ancient Synagogue at Beth Alpha Revisited - David Landau

The Blessed Date Palm - Anayat Durrani

Astrology and Judaism in Late Antiquity – Lester Ness

Drawing Down The Sky by Barry Carroll: (www.luckymojo.com/drawingdownsky.html)

Selected Websites

Assyria
www.ashur.com
www.assyrianfoundation.org/genetics.html
www.zyworld.com/Assyrian/Assyrian%20sacred%20tree%20of %20life.htm
http://cavemanart.com/osroene/abgar.htm

India
www.hindunet.org

Jewish
www.bibleorigins.net/AsherahAsherim.html
www.acsu.buffalo.edu/~vcp2/hebrew.htm
www.jhom.com/topics/seven/menorah.html
www.furman.edu/~mcknight/jer1.jpg
www.smoe.org/arcana/diss.html

Kabbalah
www.digital-brilliance.com/kab/link.htm
http://en.wikipedia.org/wiki/Kabbalah

Kurds

www.kurdistanica.com

www.xs4all.nl/~tank/kurdish/htdocs/his/orig.html

Robert Temple

www.robert-temple.com

www.abc.net.au/rn/science/ss/stories/s227039.htm

Trees

altreligion.about.com/library/weekly/aa102902a.htm

www.suite101.com/article.cfm/islam_in_the_us/37036

www.utopiasprings.com/date.htm "Tree of Faith: Date Palms of
Arabia"

Timeline

Before reading this list, it may be helpful to study the general historical accounts of ancient Iraq in Georges Roux's definitive *Ancient Iraq* Penguin Books, London, 3rd edition 1992; and that given by David Rohl in his *From Eden To Exile: The Epic History of the People of the Bible* Arrow Books, London, 2002. These writings are both thorough and gripping for the general reader.

BC(BCE)

5th mill.	Eridu founded, oldest city of Sumer
4th mill.	Nineveh (modern Mosul), early Assyrian city
c.3750	First evidence of cotton weaving. Mohenjo-Daro, India.
c.3400	First evidence of wheel-made pottery. Sumeria.
c.3200-1600	Indus Valley civilization
c.3200-2340	Cities in Mesopotamia
c.3200	Wheeled transport develops in Mesopotamia.
c.3200	Lunar calendar in Mesopotamia
c.3200	Cuneiform in Sumeria.
c.3000-2000	Anthropomorphic religion in Mesopotamia
c.2700	Megalithic culture in Europe falters, new activity in Near East
2334-c.2200	Akkadian Empire founded by Sargon
c.2200-1800	Abraham, Isaac, Jacob? Origin of the Jews
c.2000-1800	Mathematical advances in Old Babylonia
c.2000-1600	Old Babylonian Empire
c.2000	Horse introduced to W. Asia
c.2000	"Personal" religion develops in Mesopotamia
c.1900	Epic of Gilgamesh in Mesopotamia.
c.1830	First Babylonian Empire
c.1790	Babylonian Law Code of Hammurabi

c.1600-1200	Hittite Empire in Asia Minor (Anatolia)
c.1600	Invention of alphabet. Venus tablet of King Amisaduqa.
c.1550	Kassites overthrow Babylonians
c.1500-500	Arrival of the Aryans and development of Vedic society (India)
c.1400	Alphabet of Phoenicians, Assyria becomes independent state
c.1250	Moses unites Hebrews in worship of Yahweh
c.1250	Shalmaneser I of Assyria reduces Mitanni (Kurds) to a province, builds Nimrud
c.1200's	Abstract Late Assyrian Tree features in art
c.1200's	Moses leads Hebrews from Egypt to Palestine
c.1200-1025	Hebrew occupation of Canaan
c.1250	Trojan War
c.1200-800	Vedas in India
c.1100	Tiglath-Pileser I raises Assyrian power to new heights
c.1025-933	Unified Hebrew monarchy under Saul, David, and Solomon (Temple)
c.1000	David creates nation of Israel, Mul Apin written in Babylonia
c.1000	Rise of caste system in India
933-722	Kingdom of Israel (north)
933-586	Kingdom of Judah (south)
9th cent.	Aramaean Bedouin nomads become majority in Assyria
c.800-600	Upanishads in India
c.750-612	Height of Assyrian Empire
c.750-550	Hebrew prophetic revolution
c.750-400	Astronomical observation and record-keeping by New Babylonians
734	Tiglath-Pileser invades Palestine
733	Assyria takes large territories from Israel

724	Shalmaneser V marches against Hoshea of Israel
721	Assyria destroys northern kingdom of Israel, Judah pays tribute
701	King Sennacherib conquers coastal cities of Israel
c.700	Clear glass appears in the Near East.
669-626	King Ashurbanipal of Assyria, Library contains Mul Apin star list
652	Start of astronomical diaries in cuneiform
c.625	Zoroaster formulates world's first dualistic religion in Persia, using winged disc symbol like that of Ashur
612	Peak of Assyrian Empire, controls much of Middle East
612-539	New Babylonian Empire
609	Assyria loses Harran and disappears from history
c.600	Deuteronomic code
586	Nebuchadnezzar conquers Jerusalem, destruction of Solomon's Temple, people of Judah deported to Babylon
573	Ezekiel's visions while in captivity
c.569-c.475	Pythagoras of Samos, founds school in Italy
c.563-483	Life of Gautama, the Buddha
556	Nabonidus, an Aramaean from Harran, becomes last King of Babylon
539	Conquest of Babylon by Persians, Cyrus deposes Nabonidus
539-450	Judaeans return to Jerusalem, start building Zerubbabel's Temple
525	Cambyses, the Persian ruler, conquers Egypt
c.450	Hebrew Song of Songs
c.400 B.C.E.	

-70C.E.	Hebrew prophetic revolution
334-323	Conquests of Alexander the Great
327	Alexander conquers Persia and Palestine
323	Death of Alexander, division of his empire
190-120	Hipparchus makes advances in astronomy, discovers precession
2nd cent.	Pergamon, Asia Minor, first scene of Mithras as bull-slayer
187	Qumran Community (produces Dead Sea Scrolls)
166	Revolt of Maccabees
165-63	Israel independent under the Maccabees
63	Romans conquer Israel
6	Probable birth of Jesus
AD(CE)	
1st cent.	Assyrians converted to Christianity by St Thomas (?)
33	Crucifixion of Jesus
37	Birth of Josephus
64	Jewish revolt at Masada
66	Completion of Herod's Temple, war breaks out
70	Romans destroy Qumran, Jerusalem and Herod's Temple
86	Assyrians bring Christianity to China
c.100	Merkavah mysticism
132	Second Jewish Revolt
2nd cent.	Ptolemy the astronomer at Alexandria, Egypt
c.200	Sepher Yetzirah written down
6th cent.	Babylonian Talmud (commentaries) and Torah (Bible)
11th cent.	Kabbalah first named by Spanish mystic Solomon Ibn Gabriol
12th cent.	Bahir published
1275-1305	The Zohar written down in Spain by Rabbi M.

	De Leon
c.1290	Jewish text *Shaare Orah* written by Rabbi R. Gikatila in Spain, later translated as *Portae Lucis*
1415	First known Tarot cards in Northern Italy.
1463-94	Giovanni Pico della Mirandola, originator of Christian Cabala
1516	Publication of *Portae Lucis*, first book with Sephirothic Tree illustration
1517	Reuchlin writes *On the Art of Kabbalah* to persuade the Pope
1527-1608	Dr John Dee, cabalist, records Enochian angel conversations
16th-17th cents	Golden age of Kabbalah at Safed, Galilee
1534-72	Rabbi Isaac Luria at Safed in Israel, synthesises Hebrew Kabbalah into Lurianic Kabbalah.
1608	Lippershey invents telescope
20th century	Assyrians the only national group still speaking Aramaic, the language of Jesus, in northern Iraq

Endnotes

1   Baigent: *Omens of Babylon* Arkana, London, 1994 pp.176-177 and Opsopaus: *Guide to Pythagorean Tarot* Llewellyn, St. Paul, MN, 2001, pp.6,9. Baigent's *Omens* was cited as one of the recommended reading texts to those students I led on "astro-tours" of the British Museum. I understand with great pleasure that it may be republished.

2   Baigent op.cit. pp.99 and 171.

3   Rawlinson 'On the Birs Nimrud, or the Great Temple of Borsippa' *Journal of the Royal Asiatic Society* 18, London, 1861, p.17, cited by Baigent at p.154.

4   Baigent, op cit.

5   Parpola's article (from Journal of Near Eastern Studies *JNES* Vol. 52(2) Chicago, 1993) is cited extensively in the central chapters of my book, and was accessed at the School of Oriental Studies, London.

6   Livingstone, *Mystical and Mythological Explanatory Works of Assyrian and Babylonian Scholars,* Oxford, 1986, p.260 cited at Baigent p.142.

7   The Law of Attraction is explained in the popular book "Ask and It is Given" by Esther & Jerry Hicks, Hay House Publishing, Carlsbad, California, 2004.

8   Opsopaus, op.cit. p.9

9   A. Kaplan *Sefer Yetzirah: The Book of Creation*, Weiser, revised edition, York beach, Maine, 1997, p.xvii.

10   P. Berresford Ellis, *A Brief History of the Druids* Robinson, London 2002, pp.174-175

11   Opsopaus, op.cit. pp.21-22.

12   Wolkstein & Kramer *Inanna Queen of Heaven* Harper & Row, New York, 1983, p.116.

13   Baigent op.cit. p.28

14   Wolkstein & Kramer op.cit. p.118

15 Berlitz C. *The Mystery of Atlantis* Panther Books, Frogmore, St Albans, 1977 pp.150-151

16 D G White *Kiss of the Yogini* Chicago Press, Chicago, 2003 pp.28-29

17 See also Ellis op.cit. at p.123

18 See Chapter 2 of C. Penglase *Greek Myths & Mesopotamia* Routledge, London 1994

19 Black & Green, *An Illustrated Dictionary of Gods Demons & Symbols of Ancient Mesopotamia* BMP, London, 1998 p.27; and Bienkowski & Millard *Dictionary of the Ancient Near East* BMP, London 2000 p.3

20 Black & Green op.cit. p.27

21 Opsopaus op.cit. p.10

22 Kaplan op.cit. at p.23

23 See further Ellis op.cit at p.164 for a nuanced view

24 Ellis op.cit. at p.167

25 See Chapters XI onwards of Kabbalah Unveiled at "The Greater Holy Assembly" translated in Mathers, Penguin Arkana, London, 1991 from p.134

26 Black & Green op.cit. p.37 and Bienkowski & Millard op.cit. p.36

27 Bienkowski & Millard op.cit. at p.282

28 Bienkowski & Millard op.cit. p.322

29 See *The Absent Mother: Restoring the Goddess to Judaism and Christianity* ed. by A. Pirani, Mandala, London, 1991

30 See Wolkstein & Kramer op.cit. *passim* and Black & Green op.cit. at p.108 and Bienkowski & Millard op. cit. at p.156

31 See *The Date Palm* by Hilda Simon, Dodd Mead, New York, 1987 *passim* and www.utopiasprings.com/date.htm "Tree of Faith: Date Palms of Arabia"

32 Bienkowksi & Millard op.cit. p.96

33 Ditto p.169

34 Ditto pp.301-302

35 Princeton University Press, Princeton, New Jersey, 1991

36   Black & Green op.cit. p.118

37   Wolkstein & Kramer op.cit. from p.3 onwards

38   See *The Date Palm* by Hilda Simon, Dodd Mead, New York, 1987 and www.utopiasprings.com/date.htm "Tree of Faith: Date Palms of Arabia"

39   "2000 year old seed sprouts in Israel" by S. Erlanger of New York Times, http://seattletimes.nwsource.com/html/nationa-world/2002331346_datepalm12.html (accessed at Seattle Times on 4 July 2010)

40   See Chapter 7 *Myths of Aphrodite* in C. Penglase op.cit. which explores parallels between Greek and Mesopotamian divinities

41   See for example Science Daily, April 3, 1998 and Wendorf & Schild, *Holocene Settlement of the Egyptian Sahara Vol.1*, Springer, Kluwer Academic, New York, 2001

42   Baigent op.cit.

43   Baigent at pp.42-43, for example

44   Compare Baigent at p.100

45   See further in Chapter 8 of *The Origin of the Zodiac* by Rupert Gleadow, Dover, New York, 2001 reprint of 1968 edition

46   Baigent op.cit. chapter 8

47   Baigent op.cit. at pp.87-91,108,111-113, 123, 148-150, 192

48   Bienkowski & Millard, op.cit. p.105

49   Rochberg op.cit. at p.227 refers on this question to W.Mayer in a German language source, set out in her footnote. (R.Albertz ed. *Religion und Gesellschaft*, AOAT 248 (Munster, 1997) at pp.15-23

50   Baigent op.cit.

51   Baigent op.cit. Chapter 11, Bienkowski & Millard p.214 and Black & Green p.142

52   Baigent pp.156,161, Black & Green p.128 and at Bienkowski p.188

53   Baigent Chapter 12 and Black & Green p.135

54   Baigent Chapter 9 and Black & Green pp.182-184 and

Bienkowski & Millard p.263

55 Baigent pp.112-114

56 Baigent p.112

57 Baigent Chapter 10 and Black & Green at pp.108-109

58 *Drawing Down The Sky* by Barry Carroll at www. luckymojo.com/drawingdownsky.html, accessed online on 4 July 2010

59 Baigent Chapter 14 and Black & Green p.133

60 Baigent at pp.140-147

61 Bienkowski & Millard at p.239 and Baigent at pp.6-9

62 Baigent p.154 and Kollerstrom N. at p.52 of Kitson; and note the Kurdish custom of painting concentric city walls in gold, silver, blue, white, purple, red and black, reported at *The Kurds A Concise Handbook* by M. Izady, Taylor & Francis, New York, 1992 at p.263. The evidence is from *Herodotus* in respect of the garden palaces of the Medes at Ecbatana; and from Assyrian *bas reliefs* in respect of the Kurds.

63 Baigent Chapter 8

64 First published in 1948 by Faber & Faber, London

65 Published by Century, London in 2000

66 Bienkowski & Millard p.129

67 Baigent op.cit.

68 Temple op.cit at Chapter 1*passim*

69 J.B.Sellers, *The Death of Gods in Ancient Egypt*, revised edition 2003 published by lulu.com, previously published in 1992 by Penguin Books, London with significant differences

70 The alternative spelling of *delebat* is given by Walker at Kitson ed.p.9 and correlated to the planet Venus. Rochberg F. in *The Heavenly Writing* Cambridge, 2004, at p.xxv lists Venus the planet as Dilbat followed by other spellings. Rochberg (or Rochberg-Halton) is the Distinguished Professor of Near Eastern Studies at UC Berkeley.

71 See Baigent at p.70 for example

72 See Koestler A. *The Sleep Walkers* Penguin reprint, London,

1986, at pp. 50-52

73 See for example Ted Hughes *Tales from Ovid* Faber & Faber, London, 1997,which won the 1997 Whitbread Book of the Year award; he also wrote a striking Babylonian themed poem called *Horoscope* at p.64 of *Birthday Letters*, Faber & Faber, London, 1998; the Qabalistic knowledge of Hughes is revealed by Ann Skea at www.zeta.org.au/~annskea (accessed on 4 July 2010)

74 See research of Temple op.cit at pp. 175-185 and his references e.g. Alexander Thom: *Megalithic Sites in Britain* (1967) and *Megalithic Lunar Observatories* (1971) both published by Oxford

75 Baigent p.164 and p.179 for example.

76 Baigent op.cit.

77 Perhaps consult G.J. Toomer's translation of the Almagest, Princeton University Press, New Jersey, 1998, which is recommended as thoughtful by Ridpath, op.cit. p.156. I also recommend strongly *The History and Practice of Ancient Astronomy* by James Evans, Oxford, 1998 as the only book I know which gives the detail of how to do extensive practical work on ancient astronomy and hence will aid the reader in thinking like an ancient astronomer.

78 See for example Reiner E. and Pingree D. 1978,1981,1998. *Babylonian Planetary Omens,* 3 parts (Malibu, CA: Undena; and Groningen: Styx Publications)

79 See Koestler at pp. 66 ff and I. Ridpath *Star Tales* Lutterworth, Cambridge, 1988 and The Cambridge Concise History of Astronomy ed. Hoskin, Cambridge 1999 at pp.29-31

80 Allen, James Paul. 2001. "Heliopolis". In *The Oxford Encyclopedia of Ancient Egypt*, edited by Donald Bruce Redford. Vol. 2 of 3 vols. Oxford, New York, and Cairo: Oxford University Press and The American University in Cairo Press. 88–89; and Redford, Donald Bruce. 1992. "Heliopolis". In *The Anchor Bible Dictionary*, edited by David

Noel Freedman. Vol. 3 of 6 vols. New York: Doubleday. 122–123; and Mubabinge Milolo1986. *Les cosmo-théologies philosophiques d'Héliopolis et d'Hermopolis. Essai de thématisation et de systématisation*, (Academy of African Thought, Sect. I, vol. 2), Kinshasa–Munich 1987; new ed., Munich-Paris, 2004.

81 See e.g. Ridpath pp.2 ff.

82 See *The Bronze Age Computer* by A. Butler, Foulsham, Slough, 1999 *passim*

83 As reported in Ridpath at pp.3-5. He derived the theory from Roy's paper in *Vistas in Astronomy* Vol.27, 1984, p.171

84 Generally see the Cambridge Ancient History 3.1, 2nd edition (Cambridge 1982)

85 Lord Byron, line 1of *The Destruction of Sennacherib*, first published 1815, from Byron's *Works* John Murray, London, 1832 onwards

86 See for example: Christoph Baumer, *The Church of the East, an Illustrated History of Assyrian Christianity* (London and New York: I. B. Tauris, 2006); and Baum, Wilhem, and Dietmar Winkler, *The Church of the East: A Concise History* (London and New York: Routledge Curzon, 2003); quote found at http://cavemanart.com/osroene/abgar.htm - copyright Hanna Hajjar (accessed 4 July 2010)

87 Bienkowski & Millard p.205 and Baigent pp.99 and 171-2; see further P.-A. Beaulieu, The Reign of Nabonidus King of Babylon (New Haven, CN 1989) and Cambridge Ancient History 3.2, 2nd ed. (Cambridge 1991)

88 See Kabbalah by Halevi (Warren Kenton) Thames & Hudson "Art & Imagination" series ed. by Jill Purce, London, 1979 reprinted 1988, at p. 36. The whole series is admirable and includes "The Tree of Life" by Roger Cook. As *Warren Kenton*, Halevi also wrote the Astrology title in this series.

89 See p.162 of M. Izady: *A Concise Handbook of the Kurds*, Taylor & Francis, New York, USA 1992. Izady was writing as from

Harvard University's Department of Near Eastern Language and Civilisation.

90   Izady op.cit. from p.137

91   A. Kaplan, *Sefer Yetzirah: The Book of Creation*, Weiser, York Beach, Maine, revised edition, 1997

92   See P. Yogananda *Autobiography of a Yogi* 1946, using the 1998 edition published by the Self-Realisation Fellowship, Los Angeles, at p.184. The published acclaimed him as a Premavatar, or Incarnation of Love.

93   A. Watts (1966) *The Book - On the Taboo Against Knowing Who You Are*, Abacus Books, London, 1977

94   See for example G. Flood *An Introduction to Hinduism* Cambridge 1996 at Chapter 2 and further sources noted at pp. 278-279

95   See for example Ellis op.cit at p.123, and B. Cunliffe *The Celtic World*, Constable, London (1992) p.73 and *passim*

96   See for example Taylor, Timothy (1992) "The Gundestrup Cauldron" in *Scientific American* March 1992, pp. 66-71. Bergquist, A. K. & Taylor, T. F. (1987) "The origin of the Gundestrup cauldron" in *Antiquity* Vol. 61, 1987. pp. 10-24. Bober, Phyllis Fray (Jan., 1951). "Cernunnos: Origin and Transformation of a Celtic Divinity". *American Journal of Archaeology* 55 (1). Thomas McEvilley of Rice University, in "An Archaeology of Yoga" in *Res* Vol. 1, Spring 1981, pp. 44-77. Kaul, F., and J. Martens, *Southeast European Influences in the Early Iron Age of Southern Scandinavia. Gundestrup and the Cimbri*, Acta Archaeologica, vol.66, 1995 pp. 111-161. Klindt-Jensen, O., *The Gundestrup Bowl — a reassessment*, Antiquity, vol. 33, pp. 161-9. Olmsted, G.S., *The Gundestrup version of Táin Bó Cuailnge*, Antiquity, vol. 50, pp. 95-103. Cunliffe, Barry (ed.), *The Oxford Illustrated Prehistory of Europe*, NY: Oxford University Press, 1994, 400-402. Green, Miranda J., *Dictionary of Celtic Myth and Legend*. (NY: Thames and Hudson, 1992, 108-100.

97 P. Kelder *Ancient Secret of the Fountain of Youth* Doubleday, New York, 1998 and C.S.Kilham *The Five Tibetans* Healing Arts Press, Rochester, Vermont, 1994

98 Motoyama is published by Quest Books, Wheaton, Illinois, 1981

99 A. Kaplan *Meditation and Kabbalah* Jason Aronson, New York,1995

100 For example see the summary at http://www.kheper.net/ topics/chakras/chakras-earlydoctrines.htm

101 Yudelove is published by Llewellyn, St Paul, MN, 1996

102 See relevant parts of Izady at Chapter 5 and his sources; also see E. Spat *The Yezidis* Saqi Books, London, 1985; and http://www.shaikhsiddiqui.com/yazdani.html, which makes the interesting claim that the Yazdani people are identical with the Sabians of Harran, commented upon by Maimonides and discussed at Baigent p.189. The UK's Exeter University has taken the historic step of establishing a Department of Kurdish Studies which would be helpful to a full-time researcher. See also the Kurdish religion section at: http://en.wikipedia.org/wiki/Kurdish_people#Religion

103 See Bienkowski and Millard at p.150

104 See Baigent Chapter 17, and Kollerstrom's *The Star Temples of Harran* at Kitson ed. *History and Astrology*

105 Gurdjieff's *Remarkable Men* was re-published by Penguin, London in 1991. The book was filmed with Terence Stamp. Both are worthwhile.

106 See e.g. Spat op.cit.

107 D. Ulansey *Origin of the Mithraic Mysteries* Oxford, 1991

108 *Shamanism*, Princeton University Press, New Jersey, 2004 and also see his *Yoga: Immortality and Freedom* Princeton, New Jersey, 2009

109 Dr. M.Walker *Olive Leaf Extract* Kensington, New York, 1992

110 The book reference is to Lester Ness *Written in the Stars* Shangri-La Publications, Philadelphia, 1999 and the online

references (accessed 4 July 2010) are: www.abc.net.au/rn/
ark/stories/2008/2279344.htm and www.smoe.org/arcana
/diss5.html and www.stariq.com/pagetemplate/article.asp?
PageID=2607 and ftp://ftp.lehigh.edu/pub/listserv/ioudaios-
l/Articles/lnastro

111 *The Pre-biblical Origins of the Baals and the Asherim as Egyptian
Pillar Gods and Goddesses Fused to Semitic Deities in Late Bronze
Age Times (1560-1200 BCE)* - Walter Reinhold Warttig
Mattfeld y de la Torre, M.A. Ed.; accessed online at:
www.bibleorigins.net/AsherahAsherim.html

AXIS MUNDI
BOOKS

Axis Mundi Books provide the most revealing and coherent explorations and investigations of the world of hidden or forbidden knowledge. Take a fascinating journey into the realm of Esoteric Mysteries, Magic, Mysticism, Angels, Cosmology, Alchemy, Gnosticism, Theosophy, Kabbalah, Secret Societies and Religions, Symbolism, Quantum Theory, Apocalyptic Mythology, Holy Grail and Alternative Views of Mainstream Religion.